OTTO MEARS

AND THE SAN JUANS

D1516116

BY E. F. TUCKER

WESTERN REFLECTIONS
PUBLISHING COMPANY®

Lake City, Colorado

ISBN 978-1-890437-85-5

Library of Congress Control Number: 2003102304

Cover photo: Stained glass window in the Senate Chambers, State
Capitol Building, Denver, CO. Photo by Roger Whitacre Photography,
Denver, CO.

Illustrations by Lois Monarrez

Cover and text design by Laurie Goralka Design

Second Edition
Printed in the United States of America

Western Reflections Publishing Company®
P.O. Box 1149, 951 N. Highway 149
Lake City, CO 81235
(970) 944-0110
publisher@westernreflectionspublishing.com
www.westernreflectionspublishing.com

Acknowledgments

———••———

The author would like to express appreciation for the patience, effort, and invaluable assistance of Ann Hoffman, Director, and the staff at the Ouray County Historical Society Museum; Doris H. Gregory, a Ouray County historian who provided encouragement as well as materials she had available; Robert Stoufer, a local Ouray geologist who always finds time to answer questions; Edwin D. Tucker, who hand-drafted the maps; Mary Ann Dismant, Chris Reece, Barbara Staehle, and all the volunteers at the Ouray Library who patiently dealt with inter-library loan requests from all over the state of Colorado; the staff at the Saguache County Museum; and the staff at the Denver Public Library Western History Collection and the Colorado Historical Society Stephen H. Hart Library for Historical Research. Many thanks are due to P. David and Jan Smith, owners of Western Reflections Publishing Company, for their encouragement. Special thanks are due to the illustrator of this book, Lois Monarrez, who spent many hours reading, drawing, and riding uncountable miles over highways and roads in southwestern Colorado to take photographs and witness the actual locations where so many of these events took place.

I would also like to commend the patience and encouragement of my friends in Ouray and Montrose Counties who continued to ply me with questions and express their interest in this work.

My special appreciation goes to my husband, Edwin Tucker, the historian in the family, who not only provided historical background but read and edited this manuscript in its many incarnations. He chose to forego having his name as co-author, but he certainly gets half the credit. Thanks, Ed.

List of Illustrations

———

MAPS

TABLE OF CONTENTS

———

INTRODUCTION

It is said that a woman and her young daughter were driving over the Million Dollar Highway climbing south out of Ouray toward Red Mountain Pass. Hoping to teach the little girl a bit of history on the way, the mother mentioned, "A man named Otto Mears built this road."

Pretty soon the girl asked, "Did Otto Mears build the river?"

"No," said her mother, "Mother Nature built the river."

A little later the girl asked, "Did Otto Mears build the mountains?"

"No, Mother Nature built the mountains."

"Did Otto Mears build the trees?"

"No, Mother Nature built the trees."

"But Otto Mears did build the road?"

"Yes, Otto Mears built the road."

"Well," said the girl with a sigh, "I bet Mother Nature's glad that Otto Mears finally did something!"

This perhaps apocryphal story was told by Sondra Wiseman, a local Ouray businesswoman. Under the surface, it is even more humorous because as one begins to look into the matter of "what Otto Mears built," the output becomes mind-boggling. The accomplishments pile up — his trade businesses, his political contacts, his agricultural ventures, his work with the Ute Indians, his roads, his railroads, his newspapers, his mines — until one begins to wonder how one man could possibly have "built" so much in one lifetime. Charles Tarbell of Saguache, Colorado, spoke in 1927 of his friend, Otto Mears:

> *Mr. Mears is a man who always said 'I can'; and he did. In Southwestern Colorado he built the first sawmill; built the first grist mill; planted the first crop of wheat in Saguache county; owned the first thrashing machine; built the first road; was the first Treasurer of Saguache County; carried the first mail into Ouray; dug the first irrigation*

ditch (the head of the famous San Luis Ditch; later sold to the present company for $36,000). And he built the first telegraph line in Colorado — a wire on iron posts from Fort Garland to the Cantonment above Montrose, in 1879. [1]

Any biographer of Otto Mears, then, is presented with an enormous organizational problem. Mears' trading led directly to his building toll roads. His newspapers touted Saguache, Ouray, and other new towns, to bring in more business across his toll roads for his hardware stores. His political contacts enhanced his ability to work with the Utes and vice versa. His railroads helped move his goods to distribution points, haul out ore from mines and deliver it to his own and others' mills, and bring in passengers to visit the beauty of southwestern Colorado. Yet he used dirty politics to fight hard and sometimes viciously to prevent unionization of his railroad workers. Throughout it all is intermixed the complex character of the man who not only made it all possible but also often highly successful.

Although Otto Mears' life obviously progressed through stages, Mears was one of those people who seemed to be able to do everything at once, so the use of a purely chronological organization to describe his life didn't seem very effective. Therefore, this author has chosen to try to move chronologically overall, but within that chronology, to present the high points of Mears' life more or less topically. The hope is that the reader will thereby gain a picture of Mears the man, a man of his times, and a man beyond his times.

Not only was Otto Mears' life complex, but his personality was too. He was neither hero nor villain, though he has been called both — by a few, practically a saint, and by many a dastard and a scoundrel. Mears has been called eccentric, visionary, impetuous, indefatigable, sympathetic, brilliant, and inventive. He has also been called cunning, lying, cheating, ambitious, greedy, power-hungry, and self-serving. And he was all of these, as well as a strongly loyal family man (though he was rumored to be promiscuous); a man of his word (though he used bribery of politicians on a regular basis to gain his ends); one of the first businessmen in the West to institute profit sharing with his employees in his mines (yet he used every weapon in his political arsenal to fight labor regulations from the unions or the government); and a friend to the Ute Indians and fluent in their language, and a good personal friend of Chief Ouray (but a supporter of the forces that pushed the Utes out of Colorado). He was most of all, perhaps, simply a man intimately involved in the development of the Saguache and San Juan Mountain areas of southwestern Colorado in the latter part of the nineteenth century. His story is also a story of a region and an era.

An article in the *Empire Magazine* of the *Denver Post* summed up Otto Mears' life as one of a person with a "finger in every pie," uneducated, underprivileged, a poor immigrant who built a fortune. The authors said that Mears was "distinguished by one outstanding characteristic — it never occurred to him that he couldn't get any kind of job done." [2]

Helen M. Searcy in her chapter on Otto Mears in *Pioneers of the San Juan Country* said that southwestern Colorado owed its development more to Otto Mears' pioneering spirit than to any other man. "No history of the State," she said, "could be written without him as one of the chief actors on the stage of the pioneer and creative period." [3]

Chapter 1

Work or Get Out!

"The child is father of the man," Wordsworth said. Trying to psychoanalyze a historical figure is risky business, even though the subject isn't apt to come back and tell us that our evaluation was wrong. In any case, psychoanalysis is not the intent here. The childhood and youth of Otto Mears clearly laid a foundation for his later life, and it is therefore interesting to see the common themes that began early on and ran consistently through his life.

Late in his life, in 1926, Otto Mears dictated his autobiography to the secretary of Arthur M. Ridgway, the Superintendent of the Rio Grande Southern Railroad.[1] Today we would like to know a great deal more about his early life — What was his family like? What memories did he have of his parents? What was life like in Russia in the middle of the nineteenth century? But we don't have that information from Otto Mears. He covered the period of his life between birth and age eleven in a mere fifteen sentences. Mears began, "I was born May 3, 1840, in Kurland, Russia. My father died when I was a year old. He was born in England. My mother was born in Russia, or Kurland, as it was called, and died when she was forty years old."* Mears' mother was Jewish, which by Jewish law made Otto Mears Jewish as well. Michael Kaplan[2] wrote that Mears' English father was also Jewish. These tantalizing hints are about all we know of Mears' earliest background.

Kurland (now Latvia) was a province of Russia near the Baltic Sea. At that time, there weren't many Jews in Russia, as the Jewish population did not begin to soar in the Russian provinces until well after Russia annexed Poland in 1831. The infamous Russian terrorism against the Jews didn't begin until much later, and in any case, Otto Mears left Russia before 1850.

Mears' mother died before he was three years old, and he was taken in by her brother, who already had twelve children. Mears com-

---

* Otherwise unattributed quotations in this chapter are taken from Mears' memoirs as given in Williamson, *Otto Mears*.

mented that his uncle and cousins did not like him, and the uncle surely did not need yet another mouth to feed. This difficult arrangement lasted for only half a dozen years when Mears was sent to England on a vessel loaded with lumber, to an uncle on his father's side of the family. Mears was only nine years old at this time. Kaplan suggests that perhaps Mears ran away rather than being sent.[3] This may seem unlikely for a boy only nine years old, but when we look at the rest of Mears' life, we begin to realize that his running away clear across a continent might indeed have been possible.

In England, Mears traveled on what he said was the first train he ever rode, in search of his English relatives. He must have found someone, for from England he was sent by an uncle on a sailing vessel "loaded with Irish people," to New York City. He sailed alone for the duration of the six-week voyage, except, he said, for "the kind attention of an elderly lady passenger and the captain" of the ship. Another relative in New York kept him for a year and then sent him on to California to reside with one of his father's four brothers living there. This last trip involved another long sea voyage, travel across the Isthmus of Panama in a dugout and by horseback, and then an additional voyage by ship to San Francisco, traveling once more in the company of an older woman.

Eleven-year-old Otto Mears arrived in the boom town of San Francisco in 1851, after a remarkably adventurous life story to-date. This was only two years after the gold rush to California had been ignited by the gold discovery at Sutter's mining camp on the American River and fueled by reports of unimaginable wealth for the taking. In the midst of this "wild west" atmosphere, Mears discovered that the last of his paternal uncles had left the American West and emigrated to Australia. The older woman from the ship arranged for the young man to stay at the boarding house where she had a room. The boarding house proprietor, seemingly a man of business himself, told Mears to "work or get out."

Mears said that he never entered a classroom after he was ten, and very seldom before that. He had no time or financial means for education, and he immediately went to work, day and night, selling ice cream and newspapers in the wharf and dock district called the Barbary Coast. San Francisco's Barbary Coast was named after the pirate strongholds of the Mediterranean, for the San Francisco docks were places of saloons and gambling houses, with thievery, violence, and piracy in all imaginable forms. What can we say about this lad on his own in a strange country, a strange new city, with no family or adult supervision? He must have been tough — he survived; he even thrived. Mears at age eleven already demonstrated a sharp wit and quick understanding as well as a penchant for hard work.

The young boy Otto Mears was not utterly abandoned or isolated in California. There were still friends of his father's family to help him, for in 1853 a visiting merchant from Walkerville, California, a friend of Mears' family in Europe, offered him a job in his Walkerville store. Young Mears learned tinsmithing from another family friend. Later he worked for a dairyman, milking cows and driving the loaded wagon to town. These early experiences provided good background training for his later enterprises in trade and storekeeping. He left Walkerville after suffering a back injury loading the milk wagon, and he returned to San Francisco. Mears, already smart in the ways of money, was even then saving from his meager wages, but unfortunately he was robbed in a San Francisco boarding house where as many as a dozen people would all sleep in the same room. He found work at a hotel to earn enough money for passage to Sacramento and back to Walkerville.

Mears always built and used relationships with others to help him capture his goals. He never appeared to adopt the self-sufficient, independent, go-it-alone attitude which has been attributed to so many who developed the West. In Walkerville again, a chance acquaintance led to a new direction for Mears' life. He met a young man whose experiences, tales, and speculations piqued Mears' interest in the mining regions of California and Nevada. It can fairly be said throughout Mears' life that where there was money to be made, Mears would be interested. This meeting occurred in about 1859, ten years after the California gold rush had begun, and the mines were booming. Young Mears and his new friend spent months traveling to the mining areas, well fed on the abundant meals provided by the mine owners to lure the laborers they needed for the hard, dirty, and dangerous work.

Mears began to invest in the mines, a potentially lucrative business in these early gold boom days. Mark Twain, in his book *Roughing It*, which vividly described Twain's adventures in the developing West, told how even men with very little capital could buy shares in the hundreds of speculative mines started in these boom days. Even though the results of Mears' tentative investments in mining were mixed, he continued to learn. It was in Nevada that Mears discovered that the prospectors all seemed to be poor, whereas the people with ready cash were, he said, "the store and saloon keeper, and the teamster and the freighter." This observation can be confirmed by many instances from those days. For example, when H.A.W. Tabor and his first wife Augusta went to the mining camps in Leadville, it was their store and Augusta's laundry business and bakery that sustained the family until Tabor was lucky enough to strike it rich. Very few prospectors ever found the mother lode.

By mid-1860, just as he turned twenty-one, Mears was again back in San Francisco. He applied for U.S. citizenship, took out naturalization papers, and cast his first vote for Abraham Lincoln.[4] Curiously, there also exists, in the files of the Colorado Historical Society, a copy of different naturalization papers issued to Otto Mears in Saguache in 1877.

On the 14th of August, 1861, Mears enlisted in the Union Army and was assigned as a Private to Company H of the First Regiment of California Volunteers, consisting of 101 men, mostly miners. Mears gave his occupation as a "tinner."

Army pay was fifty dollars a month. The enlisted Union soldier at that time was given a minimal kit — a uniform, knife, fork, spoon, and a muzzle-loader musket. The rifled-barrel musket was the newest development in weaponry, replacing the smooth-bore musket. Because officers tended to continue to use tactics suitable to the limitations of the smooth-bore musket, for a while the new technology turned many a battle into a bloody slaughter. The rifled-barrel musket was much more accurate and had a greater range than the smooth-bore. Tactics that had been developed for the smooth-bore brought opposing forces so close together that the new accuracy of the rifled barrel enabled them to kill one another with much greater effect.

The most common item of the soldier's diet, North or South, was hardtack or "Army bread." This substance was a quarter-inch-thick, square cracker made of unleavened flour. Some men joked that their only protein came from the worms in the hardtack, and some said that it was so hard, it must have been baked fifteen years before during the Mexican War. Just before his discharge three years later, Otto Mears was assigned to the task of baking bread for the troops.

The *Regimental Description Book* describes Mears as having "black eyes, black hair, dark complexion, standing 5 feet and 5-1/2 inches in height and weighing 150 pounds."[5] David Lavender, describing an older Mears said, "He looked colorless: undersized, scraggly-bearded, dark of complexion. But life had honed him down, both physically and mentally, until he was as sharp and as resilient as the stub end of a piece of baling wire."[6]

In 1862, Mears' Company was transported by steamer to Los Angeles, where they began their march to New Mexico. Mears and Company H were involved in the battles at Valverde and Pigeon's Ranch that helped prevent the Confederacy from gaining control of the southwestern United States. Company H was not involved, however, in the major defeats dealt to the Confederates by Texas troops in the 1861 battles at Apache Pass and Glorieta Pass. Major John Chivington (of later infamy at the 1864 Sand Creek Massacre) additionally burned the Confederate supply lines. The California Volunteers, Mears among them, played their part, but were left out of, or were fortunate enough to avoid, the heaviest Civil War action in the Southwest. In 1863, Company H reinforced Kit Carson's troops who were fighting the Navajos in New Mexico.

On August 31, 1864, Otto Mears was discharged from the Army near present-day Las Cruces, New Mexico, after serving three years and seventeen days. He and his friends Isaac Gotthelf and Fred Walsen hired an ox team and wagon and set out to the north to make their fortunes.

That Pyramid of Enterprise

O tto Mears left the Army with a good amount of cash. During the Navajo campaign, Mears' quartermaster gave him the assignment of furnishing bread to the troops. Mears and his assistants camped about 150 miles west of Albuquerque, New Mexico, and built "Mexican ovens" to bake the bread. The Union Army supplied a pound of flour for each pound of bread, more than was needed, so Mears sold the extra flour for a personal profit of $1,500.[1] When Otto Mears returned to civilian life in 1864 near Las Cruces he received the $200 bonus granted to each of the California Volunteers to add to his stake made from profits on bread baking. California voted to supply volunteers their discharge money in gold, which was worth twice as much as greenbacks, so it actually amounted to $400. A third addition to his economic stake, some say, came from Mears being mustered out with considerable winnings from the endless poker games played among the troops of the Union Army. He played well — poker became a lifelong passion.

Mears and his former Army companions made their way north to Santa Fe on the old Mexican trail from El Paso. By oxcart, the young men would have needed six to eight weeks for the 300-mile journey, and even more if they stopped to work along the way. In Santa Fe, Mears got into the merchandising business again, having made a connection with the German Jewish community, which had been included among the first American traders in the area. By 1850 Jewish merchants and traders were well established in Santa Fe and there were three or four hundred Jews in New Mexico by the end of the Civil War.[2] It seems natural that Otto Mears would turn to the Jewish community, of which he was a member by birth, to begin to establish himself. He reported how he got started:

> . . . *I went to work with Elsberg and Amberg at Santa Fe. Staab Brothers had two stores, and the one at Santa Fe was large and rich. The soldiers were still there doing a great*

deal of business with them. Staab Brothers sent for me and asked me if I would like to open a store there. They said I seemed to know all about the business. They would furnish me all the supplies and my name, not theirs, would be over the door, as they didn't want the other merchants to know who opened the store.[3]

Soon tired of working for others, Mears decided to take another offer from the Staab Brothers and accept a loan with which to start his own store in Santa Fe. He moved this store to Conejos, Colorado, in 1865.

In the early 1860s flour was very much in demand in the new territory, and mills were scarce. The prospectors who needed flour for their biscuits and bread, which were staple food in the camps in those days, discovered in 1860 that they couldn't get flour anywhere in the San Luis Valley. At Fort Garland, the nearest U.S. Army post to Conejos, the Army was paying the high price of twenty dollars for a hundred pounds of flour and eighty dollars for a thousand feet of lumber. There was an obvious need, and Mears jumped in to meet it. He went into partnership with Lafayette Head to start up and to operate both a flour mill and a sawmill.

John Lawrence was another young man at Conejos looking for an opportunity. While Mears was running his store, Lawrence was freighting and trading for Colonel John Francisco and Ceran St. Vrain. These two young men, Mears and Lawrence, could see the extravagant prices the U.S. Army was paying for lumber, flour, and beef, and they searched for and found suitable land for wheat farming and cattle ranching near present-day Saguache, Colorado, where they moved in the summer of 1866. They continued to work together, but also frequently fought with each other, for the next decade. Mears became a Republican, Lawrence a Democrat. Mears branched out into roads and railroads; Lawrence stayed in ranching. Mears expanded his economic and political influence into southwestern Colorado, Denver, and even nationally, while Lawrence stayed pretty close to Saguache, developing one of the large ranching outfits in the district.

While equipping and running a store, growing and milling wheat, and developing roads, Mears demonstrated another trait that would characterize him all his days — when he didn't have the capital for a venture, he found a partner. Such were his business acumen and persuasive ways, that he rarely had trouble finding someone to go into business with him. In 1866 he bought government land near what would become Saguache, which he planted with more wheat as well as pota-toes and oats, and in the same year, he moved his gristmill and his home north to that area. Mears then moved his store from Conejos to Saguache. To bring in goods, he started operating pack trains from Denver to Saguache, by way of La Veta Pass. Packing rates on those old trails were generally ten cents a pound.

In 1867, Fred Walsen, another of Mears' friends from the Army who was discharged with Mears and Gotthelf in Las Cruces, came to the area to homestead. Walsen soon transferred title of his ranch to Mears for a $1,000 loan. Within a month, Mears had re-mortgaged the combined Mears-Walsen ranches, with farm equipment, wagons, and oxen teams, for $4,450, the first mortgage recorded in the Saguache County Court House. In February 1868, Mears sold part of the ranch and subsequently paid off the mortgage. He later sold the remainder of the ranch to his other Army companion, Isaac Gotthelf.

As is often the case, local families and historians debate the origin of the name of Saguache. Allen Nossaman, in *Many More Mountains*, says it is a Ute word for "Blue Earth." Mears said it means "Blue Spring." Mears later claimed the word "Saguache" [pronounced *Suh-watch*] was misspelled and that it resulted from a clerical error. It was his intention [as a founder of the town] to name the area "Swatch" . . . . Even after the spot was officially called Saguache, Mears referred to it as "Swatch."[4]

In 1867, Mears brought the first threshing machine into the area. It was an innovation that demonstrated two more aspects of his lifelong character — his openness to new ideas and technology, and his ability to deal with all sorts of people of very different cultures and languages, including his own employees. The Mexican workers didn't trust this new-fangled machine, claiming that it was stealing their wheat and that at best, it was inefficient and wasteful. But Mears won their confidence, and soon they were using it willingly. Mears convinced them that even though hand threshing lost less grain, the economy of scale of the machine, as well as the reduction in physical labor, were worth the small loss of grain.

In 1867, Mears, John Lawrence, and others incorporated the town of Saguache. An advertisement for the town of Saguache can be found in the March 9, 1867, edition of the *Santa Fe Weekly Gazette* — today we would surely take issue with it based on modern "truth in advertis-ing" principles:

> *Saguache occupies the southern* [sic] *portion of the San Luis Valley, and for fertility of soil, general productiveness, and*

*salubrity of climate, it has no equal, and is universally rec-
ognized as "the garden spot" in Colorado. Under such favorable circumstances, it is not to be wondered at that
"squatters" are daily arriving from all parts, to inhabit, and
permanently occupy, that rich and exciting locality.*[5]

As well as running his store, expanding it to a branch store in Del
Norte at the southern end of the San Luis Valley, and getting involved in
the local affairs of the area, Mears was doing some freighting, as he had
four yoke of oxen and four wagons. He freighted goods from Denver
and even from Santa Fe, no doubt to supply his own stores as well as to
transport goods for others.

Another major thread in Otto Mears' life appeared at this time —
almost immediately after arriving in Saguache, Otto Mears became
involved in politics. His reasons do not appear to be either a quest for
power or any ideological factor. In fact, in an era when one's political
party was practically as firm a commitment as one's religion, Mears was
a Republican in Colorado, later a Democrat in Maryland and Louisiana,
for a while a Populist and a "Fusionist," and finally a Republican again.
In spite of Michael Kaplan's assertion that Mears had a lust for power, [6]

Otto Mears' first home and store in Saguache, Colorado.

it is more defensible to believe that Otto Mears' primary motivation in life was to make money — political life, for him, was simply a means to that end. With political power wielded behind the scenes, friendships with and favors owed by highly placed political figures, Mears could get the laws, regulations, and official approval needed for him to be successful in his money-making projects.

John Lawrence had been lobbying the Colorado Territorial Assembly as early as 1866 to cut off a piece of Costilla County to create the then virtually uninhabited Saguache County. When Lawrence succeeded and Saguache County was formed, Territorial Governor Alexander Cummings appointed Lawrence County Judge for the new Saguache County, and Mears was appointed, and later elected, County Treasurer for three terms. The job of the county treasurer was to collect taxes, and since the populace had little ready cash, they often paid in goods that the treasurer would sell for the taxes due. Mears would receive furs, buckskins, or farm produce, sell these, and then turn the proceeds over to the Colorado Territorial Treasurer in payment of county taxes.

Mears was Saguache County's Republican representative to the Territorial Convention in 1870, and soon became a member of the Republican State Central Committee. By the time Colorado became a state in 1876, Otto Mears had already long been deeply enmeshed in Colorado political life.

To try to ensure that the town of Saguache was declared the county seat over the protests of citizens of the other tiny communities in the new county, Mears used some questionable methods to gain votes for his hometown. Even though buying votes was strictly against the law, it was said that Otto Mears offered John Lawrence $500 if Lawrence would deliver the votes of the local Mexicans, with whom Lawrence had some influence as he had a Mexican wife, to ensure that "Saguache City" would be chosen as county seat of the new county. Lawrence held out for $700. When Mears refused to raise his price, Lawrence had Mears indicted for trying to buy votes. Otto Mears responded by having Lawrence indicted for trying to sell them, and the contest ended in a draw.[7] In spite of this and other differences, Mears and Lawrence remained friends.

Holding the designation of county seat was important both politically and economically for a town. Townspeople were not above considerable chicanery to assure that their town would get or retain the county seat. For example, Leland Feitz, in his book, *Creede, Colorado Boom Town*, mentions:

> *In 1893, Mineral County was established, carved out of parts of Hinsdale, Rio Grande, and Saguache Counties. Wasson, three miles south of Creede, was designated county seat. A. H. Wasson, founder of the rival town, built the court- house himself. But, the good people of Creede were not about to go along with that plan. They did not like "that town in the cow pasture," as they called it. They felt the county seat should be in Creede and on a dark night a number of Creede's people went to Wasson and hauled the county records to their city. Later the frame courthouse itself was chopped into several pieces and moved to Creede.*[8]

In Ouray County, two conflicting Boards of Trustees fought for control of the county, the old Board even hiding the county records so that the newly elected Board could not find them.

A classic, entertaining, and informative contemporary history of the Saguache area and the time is Anne Ellis's *The Life of an Ordinary Woman*. Ellis's family moved to the Rocky Mountains when she was a small child. She grew up and lived most of her life in the mining camps and small towns of Colorado. She moved to Saguache some years after Otto Mears had moved away, but she heard plenty of stories about him from the residents. For example, regarding Mears' politics:

> *From town, going over and through the mountains to Shirley, there was, and still is, a toll road built by Otto Mears, the Pathfinder, and he was a sure-enough road builder! Some of this road is very good yet, and, where it is graded on the high mountain sides, it still winds in and out among the trees. Nature seems to know it for a good job and does not try to cover it. I have heard that Mears built this road before an election — not that a road was needed especially, but he did need votes.*[9]

Later Anne Ellis added:

> *At one election Otto Mears gave prospective voters hams, bacon, and sacks of flour, much better, it seems to me, than cigars or whiskey.*[10]

Colorado Territory became the State of Colorado on August 1, 1876. At the August 1876 Saguache County Republican Convention, Mears was one of three men elected as delegates to the state convention in Pueblo. He participated in organization of the party in the new State of Colorado, and was directly involved in selection of the party's candidates for Governor and Lieutenant Governor. John L. Routt, the last Territorial Governor, was a natural choice to run for Governor, and Lafayette Head, Mears' former business partner in Conejos, was selected as Republican candidate for Lieutenant Governor. Already, Mears was actively seeking to retain and foster his friendship with associates in high political places.

In November, Mears was chosen to be one of the three United States Presidential Electors by a joint session of the Colorado legislature. Mears traveled to the East Coast to carry Colorado's three electoral votes for Rutherford B. Hayes, the successful candidate from the National Republican Party.

Mears continued to be a power in the Colorado State Republican Party, enough of a power that he played a major role in the nomination of Republican candidates for office. In 1878 he successfully promoted Frederick W. Pitkin, a wealthy mining investor from Ouray County, as the Republican Party candidate for Governor of Colorado.

As became more and more evident through his life, Otto Mears did not let politics, or little else, get in the way of his business interests. In 1868, gold had been discovered in California Gulch and Granite Gulch in what would later become the Leadville Mining District. When the Army's price of flour dropped to five dollars per hundred pounds, Mears stopped sending his flour to Fort Garland and decided instead to ship it north to the new mining areas, as the miners were willing to pay double what the Army would give. In fact, this apparent setback might be seen as the opening to the activity for which he later became so well known — building roads.

The year 1873 brought a national economic downturn. It was during this troubled period that one of Mears' more notorious escapades occurred. His Saguache general store was in debt for $1500, and the primary financial investor in the enterprise, a local English expatriate named H. R. Prior, refused Mears any more advances. Mears induced a visitor, William Laddingham, to invest $1500 with him to be used in a horse raising venture. Mears used this money to pay off his creditors. Unfortunately for Mears' deal with Laddingham, however, there were no horses. Months later, when Laddingham returned, Mears managed to be out of town. In the end, Mears escaped arrest only because his friend Isaac Gotthelf interceded and provided real security, instead of fictional horses, for Laddingham's investment.

In 1874, Mears founded the first newspaper, the *Saguache Chronicle*. He hired an experienced newspaperman from Pennsylvania, David Downer, as publisher. The intent of the paper was to promote the Saguache region in every facet possible — climate, fertility, mineral wealth, and opportunity — to induce greater settlement. Only a month later, Mears, with more than half a dozen other investors, incorporated the Saguache Printing and Publishing Company to publish the *Saguache Chronicle* and to do other printing jobs as well.

In 1875, because of Mears' investment in the new Saguache and San Juan Toll Road to Lake City, as well as exciting mineral finds near Lake San Cristobal by his Lake City road contractor, Enos Hotchkiss, Mears provided capital for the founding of the new Lake City Town Company, and Mears, Hotchkiss, and Isaac Gotthelf were listed among those on the town's first board of trustees. Right away, he subsidized the foundation of a weekly newspaper, the Lake City *Silver World*. They had no building and had to put the equipment in a tent. The first issue was produced under these difficult conditions, and the editor, a Mr. Wood, crossed the range from Lake City on skis to deliver copies to the people of the town of Del Norte.[11] Lake City boomed over the next several years, boosted by the rich mineral finds in that area as well as the *Silver World's* enthusiastic advertising to the outside public. Lake City boasted a population of 2000 inhabitants only three years after its birth.

Otto Mears continued to operate his store in Saguache. Anne Ellis recounts a tale that provides humorous illustration of both Mears' business acumen and his relations with his neighbors:

> *[Otto Mears] was a man of wonderful judgment; for instance. . . he had a store in Saguache, and a pioneer woman told me "he swapped tobacco and whiskey to the Indians who would come in from the agency — no roads — galloping their horses over the chico, till they looked like waves." She also told me this story: "Once, all our husbands was out burying a man who had been killed in a drunken shooting scrape — some of them had been drinking a lot too — so us wives went up to Mears's Store . . . and we went*

in and smashed in the heads of the barrels and poured whiskey into the road. Mears never said a word, just looked on, but, lo and behold, when our husbands got their bills, they were charged with all that whiskey, between four and five hundred dollars worth. Money so scarce, too."[12]

Mears took advantage of any opportunity that he saw as having good potential for profit. Late in the 1870s, the weather turned against the farmers in the San Luis Valley, and feed was short. Ranchers in the valley had to sell many of their cattle because they hadn't been able to store up enough feed to get the stock through what turned into a heavy winter. Mears and his partners bought up around 4,000 head of cattle and sold them to the government. The cattle were driven to the Indian Agency where they were slaughtered as the needs of the Ute Indians required. Mears and his partners made a handsome profit from the bad luck of the ranchers and the needs of the Indians, by way of the U.S. government.[13] David Frakes Day in his newspaper, the *Solid Muldoon* of September 19, 1879, called Mears "That pyramid of enterprise, and prince of Rocky Mountain rustlers . . . ."

With characteristic energy, in the mid-1870s Mears became a mail contractor. Having bid on one mail route that never panned out because there weren't enough people on the route to justify it, Mears began in 1874 to deliver weekly mail from the Ute Indian Agency at Los Pinos to Saguache, a distance of forty miles, for which he was paid $432 a year from the Post Office Department. In 1875, the route was extended 100 miles to Silverton and increased to three deliveries a week, for an additional annual payment of well over twice that amount.[14] Mears arranged a network of service trails from the agency, with rest stations twenty-five miles apart for the mail carriers and their animals. In the fall, Mears also added a mail contract to Ouray. That same year, the Indian Agency was moved to the Uncompahgre Valley, south of present-day Montrose.

Mail delivery could be risky work. The story of one of the first mail carriers provides insight into how difficult and dangerous a job it could be. George W. Beckwith, who had been picked by Mears to carry mail from the Cimarron Agency in New Mexico Territory to the new Los Pinos Agency, had a horse go lame. He lassoed a wild mustang from the agency corral to break as a replacement. In the tussle, Beckwith got tangled up in the rope between his saddle horse and the mustang and was trampled to death. His grave, well cared for and marked with a hand-chiseled headstone, can still be found in a small, private cemetery on a hill above the present-day town of Colona, Colorado, near where the second Los Pinos Agency was located.

Later that winter, as the snow piled high in the San Juans, a man named Stewart Daniells, who had once delivered mail for the Hudson's Bay Company, stopped by the agency and suggested to Mears the advantages of using dog sleds in the winter. Mears was convinced, so he hired Daniells to run the sleds and Daniells immediately began training dogs.

Otto Mears in a Russian cap and heavy fur coat, for comfort in the severe San Juan winters.

To increase his profits, Mears began transporting supplies along with the mail. Unfortunately, if there was food in those supplies, the dogs would start fighting to get into the food. In addition, Ouray women who ordered hats or other finery from the East would often find them crushed by the rest of the load. They complained to the United States Post Office, and Mears was forced to carry mail and goods in separate sleds, and to better control the dogs.

In January of 1876, the weather was so cold and the snows so heavy that even the dog sleds could not get through and the mail carriers refused to make the trip. Mears announced that he would curtail service until the trails were passable. The editor of Silverton's *La Plata Miner* protested, the *Denver Tribune* picked up the story, and soon the authorities in Washington sent notice to Mears that he had to get the mail through or pay a stiff fine. Unable to convince anyone else to make the trip, Mears made it himself, both to avoid liability for the large fine he would have to pay if the mail did not get through, and probably with an element of showing off to the mail carriers that if they couldn't do it, he could. It took him three days to make the journey, with great difficulty and fatigue. At one point on the Lake Fork of the Gunnison River, he had to wade through two feet of wet snow with icy water running underneath. He managed the risky, grueling trip, and from then on, the mail was delivered on schedule.

Even though he was continually involved in other enterprises, Otto Mears retained his stores. As late as 1878, an advertisement appears in the *Saguache Chronicle* of May 23, calling attention to Mears & Co. selling a popular brand of blasting powder at $4.25 per keg.

Civilization was arriving on the frontier but settlers had little opportunity to become dull or complacent. Back in the early days of 1867 a rumor was spread that the White Mountain Utes from northern Colorado Territory were going to attack Saguache. Mears built a barricade around his house and stationed the men of the area there. The women were kept indoors where they were put to making bullets out of chunks of lead chopped up and melted over the fire and then poured into molds. Word was sent to Fort Garland, ninety miles away, for help.

More than two nights later, the infantry approached Mears' house and store, not realizing that Saguache Creek had flooded out of its banks. In the pitch darkness, the soldiers marched forward with their heavy guns and cartridge belts and fell right into the creek. The whole first line of men fell down the bank and were submerged, but they didn't cry out for fear of alerting the Utes. Therefore, the second line also tumbled into the water on top of the first.

The soaked and angry soldiers scrambled up the far bank, only to find the well-lighted stockade open and unguarded — Mears had heard earlier that the Utes had been persuaded to turn back.[15]

The story was told by Mears himself, and certainly places him in the prominent role in the tale. Mears is reported to have observed that the soldiers would have been useless anyway, with their guns and ammunition soaked.[16]

The tale is illustrative of the constant fear of attack under which the settlers lived, and the difficulty of defense in case of need. Anne Ellis reflects on her mother's dreadful fear of Indians from her crossing the country to Colorado from Missouri. Ellis adds, "I knew a woman who made this journey just before her baby was born. That baby is now an old man, and he always goes peeking around corners, sidling, slipping, and watching, in constant fear of the Indians."[17]

Frontier life was not all alarms and battles. The ordinary and the everyday were the norm, and family life, as well as business life, was the center. Otto Mears met Mary Kampfshulte at Granite, Colorado, in the mining region north of Nathrop, between present-day Salida and Buena Vista. The beautiful, dark-haired German woman had accompanied her brother to Colorado when he came for health reasons. It wasn't long before Certificate No. 6 in the records of marriages in Saguache County was issued on the 17th day of November, 1870, to Otto Mears and Miss Mary Campshettler [sic] and they were married that same day before David Goff, the Justice of the Peace. They eventually had three daughters and one son — Laura May, born in 1872; Eva, whose birth date is unknown, but she died on May 31, 1876, at the age of four and a half months; Cora, born November 25, 1879; and a son whose name we don't know, who was born January 8, 1887, and died three days later. Both Laura and Cora married, and both sons-in-law were involved in Mears' railroad businesses. Laura died childless in 1915, while Cora had four sons and died in 1948.

In the early years, Otto and Mary Mears were very close. She often accompanied him on business trips, even though these could involve riding in a wagon over rough, rutted roads, across flooded streams, and even through the territory of sometimes hostile Indians. But as the years wore on, Mary suffered health problems and as a consequence, she and Otto were more often separated. Mears developed a reputation for being a ladies' man, though apparently he always cared deeply for Mary. He was a concerned father who spent a lot of time and money on his children. Otto's and Mary's marriage lasted for fifty-four years, until Mary died in 1924.

Personal life on the frontier was not limited just to families. There was an enormous amount of socializing among the scattered settlers in the Rocky Mountain frontier. Of course they all worked hard and long, but they also visited and ate with one another and celebrated and just had fun together. John Lawrence's diary[18] is full of entries noting the gatherings of various single men and families for a supper, an evening, or even for a work party followed by food and drink. The Indians were usually not included, but the Mexicans often participated. Part of the reason for their inclusion was that John Lawrence's wife and several of the other settlers' wives were Mexican.

Celebration was found or created where it could be. John Lawrence* writes: "July 4, 1869. I went down to Mearses on horseback. While there Lilly & McBroom & also Taylor passed by coming up here. Mears and I also came up. After dinner we all went down, also Fullerton. We came to Mearses and shot off 35 rounds on the anvils to celebrate the Fourth."[19]

Another entry in Lawrence's diary hints at some of the socializing and also provides an interesting note into the economics of the day, though this was slightly later.

> *September 11, 1872. I went down below to give security for the contracts I and Mears got yesterday, being 20,000 lbs. of oats at 4 1/4¢ a lb., 1000 lbs of turnips at 3¢ per lb., 500 lbs. of beats [sic] at 5¢ per lb., 500 of parsnips and 500 of carrots at 5¢ per lb., and 1000 lbs cabage [sic] at 6¢ per lb., and 500 lbs. of onions. After I gave the security I went down . . . to the store and bet $10 on Pumfrey's horse against Uray's [Chief Ouray's] horse, and as usual lost . . . we got drunk & had a heap of talk, and knocked Francisco Chaves down. Day fine.*[20]

In 1877 Saguache County organized and held its first county fair and agricultural exhibition. Otto Mears' stock won a prize in the horse

---

* John Lawrence used his own unique spelling. That spelling has been retained in all quotations from his diary.

show.[21] Two years later, at the Fourth of July celebration in 1879, horse races were held. Saguache citizenry did not come out so well on this occasion. All the betting in the town was placed on a local favorite that had never lost a race. But that favorite was defeated by a horse owned by a traveler from Kansas who departed the area enriched by much of Saguache's cash and a few Indian ponies.[22]

There was also "church" in some form or another, hardly regular but an event worth noting in Lawrence's diary. When the Catholic priest happened by, whole batches of marriages might be legalized at one time, although the situation could be complicated when the individuals had not yet had the opportunity to receive Catholic instruction.[23] John Lawrence himself gives us an interesting view of what he found notable one October day:

> *I went down below in the morning on horseback. I seen Uray [Chief Ouray] at Godfreys. I had a long talk with him in which he told me that the Utahs made no treaty while at Washington last winter . . . . I went down to Mears. The Old Preacher was there. Mr. Ashley went up to notify the people that there would be preaching in the evening. Woodson and Fullerton came down in the evening to the preaching in the carriage. Day fine.*[24]

The "old preacher" was the Reverend John L. Dyer, familiarly called "Father Dyer" by his flock, a Methodist circuit preacher who traveled all over the Colorado Rocky Mountains, based primarily around Leadville, gathering a congregation where he could and preaching a fiery gospel to them. Late in his life, Dyer published his memoirs, and he mentions the incident described by Lawrence. At Saguache he found a few Protestants — the Mexicans were predominantly Catholics — and as was his habit, asked permission to hold a service, or "preach," as he called it, in a local home.

> *At Saguache I found a small settlement, and held a two days' meeting at the house of Mr. Ashley, a family from Kentucky. They were Baptists, and good people, but had hardly heard of a Protestant preacher being in the country. They kept me, and it seemed like home in the wilderness. On Sunday the power of God came down, and nearly all*

were in tears. The lady of the house broke out with a grand
shout, the first ever raised in the San Luis Valley . . . . We
had there a foreigner, I think of Jewish descent [almost
undoubtedly Otto Mears]. He sat near the door, and looked
first at the door, then at me, and then at the scene among
the seekers." [25]

By the late 1870s, Saguache boasted at least four churches —
Catholic, Methodist, Presbyterian, and Baptist. The latter especially
supported evangelization in the mining camps around Bonanza.
Unitarian meetings were also apparently held, as Cora Mears was bap-
tized as an infant in 1880 as a Unitarian in Saguache.

And work and trading went on even among friends and partners.
John Lawrence wrote:

> *May 12, 1869. I went down to Mearses last evening*
> *and stayed all night. In the morning I went up to Fourds.*
> *I there traded for Mearses old horse. I then went down &*
> *got him. I also got some coperas of Ashley, some sulfer of*
> *Andy Settle & some salt pieter of Harris. I got home after*
> *night. If I give the horse back to Mears when he is cured, he*
> *is to give me a two year old hiefer but if I keep him I am*
> *to pay 1500 lbs. of oats this fall. Francisco sold his jack.*
> *Godhelf was here to dinner . . . .* [26]

As we know, Mears went on to make his living in roads and railroads and mining. Lawrence built in a different direction, primarily
ranching. By 1883 it was reported that Lawrence, who had arrived six-
teen years before with little capital, now owned nearly 7,000 sheep and
cattle on his ranches. John Lawrence died February 14, 1908, at Mercy
Hospital in Denver still wearing the long red underwear that he refused
to let the nurses remove.

In early 1874, Otto Mears became involved in the fascinating mis-
adventure of Alferd M. Packer, the "Cannibal of the San Juan." In
January 1874, five prospectors who were unwilling to stay the winter at
Chief Ouray's winter camp, at the junction of the Uncompahgre and
Gunnison Rivers, made the deadly decision to accept Packer's offer to
guide them through the mountains to the Los Pinos Indian Agency.
Chief Ouray tried to discourage them, but they were determined to go

ahead. Weeks later, Packer appeared at the agency alone and asked for aid. He was allowed to recuperate there. When a second party arrived in the spring, having spent the winter comfortably at Ouray's camp, Packer's story of having been abandoned by his companions was strongly questioned. Nevertheless, he was left free of restraint.

One day, Packer entered Mears' store in Saguache and negotiated to buy a horse. The price of seventy dollars was agreed upon, but Mears refused Packer's banknotes, as Packer had a reputation for being a counterfeiter. In fact, this reputation was earned, as Packer had been jailed a short time before in Salt Lake City for passing counterfeit money.[27] Packer produced a second wallet and different notes. Mears said that his suspicions were heightened when he saw a Wells Fargo Express Company draft in the second wallet for considerable money.[28] Packer later asserted that Mears told him that he was a fool and should get out of the area.[29] It seems likely that Packer was lying about Otto Mears' comment, since Mears had refused Packer's banknotes and thus insulted Packer's veracity.

Still later, Mears sought out General Charles Adams, the Indian Agent at Los Pinos. The two men agreed to induce Packer to return to the agency where Adams had authority to detain him while an investigation was conducted. Once arrested, Packer broke down under heavy questioning and told this story: He said that his party had run out of food shortly after leaving Ouray's camp, and that members of the party had resorted to murder and cannibalism to survive. Ouray apparently had given Packer and his companions a crude map, telling them to start out up the Gunnison River to Cebolla Creek, and then to head up the Creek to the Los Pinos Agency. Packer evidently turned too early, traveled up the Lake Fork of the Gunnison instead, and this mistake led him and his ill-fated companions directly to the spot where the Packer Massacre was later discovered.

Packer claimed to have killed no one except a man named Bell in self-defense, but he admitted to having resorted to cannibalism to survive. Packer admitted that he had taken some money from the corpses before he made his way to the agency.

Two months later, after the winter snow melted, the remains of the other prospectors were found. An inquest determined that four of the men had been murdered while asleep and the fifth was killed with a blunt instrument while defending himself. Even as an order was sent to Saguache to put him on trial, Packer escaped.

Ten years later, Packer was recognized in Wyoming and General Adams was notified. The cannibal was arrested and finally brought to trial at Lake City, the county seat of Hinsdale County and near where the alleged murders had taken place. Mears testified at the trial, offering evidence against the defendant. Packer was found guilty and sentenced to death. An apocryphal but popular story states that the judge in the case, a staunch Democrat, thundered (there are variations of course): "Packer you depraved Republican son of a bitch, there were only five Democrats in Hinsdale County, and you ate them all!"

Packer's lawyers appealed to the Colorado Supreme Court on grounds that the sentence of death was illegal, as the Colorado legislature had repealed the 1870 statute for murder before Packer's crime, and had not enacted a new one until afterward. After languishing in the Gunnison County jail for three years, Packer was finally retried there for manslaughter, convicted, and sentenced to a forty-year prison term. Otto Mears stated that he was "unavailable" to testify at this second trial, so his testimony from the first trial was read into the record at the second.[30] As he went to state prison, Packer threatened revenge against Mears for his testimony.

Another fifteen years later, the *Denver Post*, probably in an attempt to increase circulation, began a campaign protesting Packer's innocence. Led by Miss Polly Pry, this campaign included considerable invective against Otto Mears.

> *But the man who, from motives of his own, testified to things he could not have known; the man who is afraid, who for nineteen years has trembled at a threat made in a moment of terrible excitement and wild rage, that man is the governor's friend. In fact, he calls himself the "governor-maker" of Colorado. I herewith present him to you: His name is Otto Mears. You all know him. He is a little old man with a shrewd face and a shifty eye, a trader who always has a new scheme and who never gets the worst of a bargain.*[31]

Alferd Packer was eventually pardoned and freed. He died six years later. His earlier threats of vengeance against Otto Mears were never carried out.

In a curious footnote to history, in the late 1990s, a reenactment of Alferd Packer's trial was held in Lake City. Jurors were chosen; evidence was presented. In this unofficial trial more than one hundred years after the fact, Alferd M. Packer was found innocent of the charges of murder.

CHAPTER 3

The Toll Road King

It was 135 miles from Conejos, Colorado, to the mining camps around what would later be called Leadville, and those miles included the trip over 9000-foot Poncha Pass. Otto Mears was hauling a wagon load of grain over the pass to Charles Nachtrieb's mill. Only a rough path existed on that route. In those days, people didn't yet put the grain into sacks, so the wagon was piled with loose grain. Not at all surprisingly, considering the condition of the trail, the wagon hit a rough spot and tipped over, spilling the grain. Mears often told the story that as he was shoveling spilled grain back into the righted wagon,

> *[Former Governor] William Gilpin came along on horseback. In 1867 he owned the Baca Grant, one hundred thousand acres of land in the San Luis Valley. He was a very able man but rather crazy. He asked me why I didn't take out a charter and build a toll road, that it would only cost me $5.00 and I could make a lot of money out of it. He said some day there would be thousands of people in San Luis Valley, and we could raise lots of things there . . . . So he told me to make a road out of that, and I started in. I did not have any regular tools for it, but I had axes and shovels, and built a road to get my wheat down [over Poncha Pass], and finally got it to Charles Nachtrieb's mill in the Arkansas Valley . . . . I went to Denver and got a charter and made a good road in 1867.[1]*

It was easy enough to incorporate a toll road company. As Mears himself said, all that a man needed for the right to construct and operate a toll road was to acquire a charter for a five-dollar fee. In the early days, this required a trip to Denver, but later on one could get such a charter from the county. This document awarded the right to operate the road as a toll road for twenty years. No map, layout, or engineering design was needed — a simple statement of the beginning and ending points and perhaps some indication of the general route were the only requirements.

The Poncha Pass Wagon Road Company was incorporated on November 8, 1870, with a capital stock of $2000 divided into 400 shares. The road would run from Poncha Pass north along Poncha Creek to its confluence with the South Arkansas River. The primary investor besides Mears was Charles Nachtrieb. The road was later extended farther north to Nathrop, to intersect the stage road between Denver and California Gulch (now Leadville), and where, not coincidentally, Nachtrieb had large holdings.[2]

Charles Nachtrieb was in some ways an utter contrast to his friend and partner Otto Mears. Nachtrieb was tall and strong, but he had a hot temper and he had great difficulty dealing with his employees. It was said around Nathrop, which he founded, that he had so much trouble with the men who worked for him that a man who could get along with Charley Nachtrieb was news in the valley. Otto Mears, small and scrawny, but with a legendary ability to get along with other men, including his own employees, was one of the few who got along with Charles Nachtrieb.

The Poncha Pass wagon road that Nachtrieb built with Otto Mears was, of course, only one of many roads cut through the mountains and valleys at that time. Toll roads were a boon, indeed a necessity, to the development of the territory. Before wagon roads existed, all goods both into and out of an area would have to be hauled by pack trains of burros or mules. In mining areas even the ore would have to be packed out on animals. Before roads were "improved" there was some wagon travel, but it was slow, laborious, and often risky. For example, in a report to the governor, Otto Mears said that the fifty-five miles of mountain trail to the Indian Agency at Los Pinos sometimes took ox-drawn wagons as much as eleven days to make the trip.[3]

What a problem transportation was in Colorado in those early times. Ore, grain, lumber, equipment, clothing, and food — it went by wagon or oxcart, and where there wasn't a wagon road for these, it went by mule or burro. A mule could carry 250 pounds upgrade and 350 down, whereas the most a burro could manage to carry was an average of 200 pounds. However, a mule had to be fed, but a burro could eke out sustenance on the scraggly grass of the mountain slopes. Mules were irascible and notoriously difficult to control, and they had to be led. Of course the "mule skinner" could ride the lead mule, but burros could only be driven.

Burros learned to go in single file only when the trail was too narrow to accommodate them as a herd. When a fork in the road appeared, dogs had to be trained to nip the burros on the side of the wrong trail, turning them toward the desired direction. Burros also did not have to be shod. Horses were used, of course, but they didn't have the surety of footing of either mules or burros, essential in these mountains, and horses had thinner skin, making them less useful in packing.

Everything that couldn't go by wagon went by pack animal. The *Leadville Chronicle* for March 15, 1881, provides one startling report on the attempts of a crew of impatient bakers heading for Aspen over the Independence Trail with their huge oven. Though the story is not directly connected with Otto Mears, it provides excellent, as well as entertaining, background to show the problems faced by freighters and the crying need for Mears and many others to build decent roads through the mountains.

> *A sled was purchased, on which the furnace was securely fastened . . . with half a dozen jacks [mules] as motive power. The trail soon narrowed to such an extent that the projecting sides of the oven stuck, and it was found necessary to excavate several feet at each side to admit its progress. At night the weary bakers slept in the oven, haunted by the faint aroma of pastry that, like the scent of roses, hung around it still . . . . Meanwhile an unexpected difficulty arose. The spring tide of travel had already set in, and several jack trains were not long in following the bakers' caravan. They were not long in catching up with it, either, and the awful fact dawned upon them that they could not pass it, but would have to linger in the rear. This filled them with sorrow and disgust, for they were in a hurry, and, like most travelers into a new mining camp, imagined if they didn't get there right away all the land would be staked off, all the trades overcrowded and all the provisions eaten up . . . . Then another and another jack train came hurrying up, and stopping at the rear of their unfortunate predecessors, inquired anxiously:*
> *"What's up?"*
> *"A G— D— pie factory is blockading the road!"*
> *"Well, why don't you push the ———— thing off?"*

"Can't do it, it's too hell-fired big!"

The oven isn't at Aspen yet, and isn't liable to be before late this week, and the pack trains still accumulate in the rear, until the road for nearly a mile is black with shivering, swearing, howling men.[4]

Wagons, pulled by up to twelve oxen or by six Percheron/Belgian-cross work horses, were preferred to mules or burros when roads were available. With the development of adequate roads, of course, came many more wagons, as wagons were more efficient than pack animals. Sometimes on narrow roads, when two wagons met, finding passing room was extremely difficult. On very steep parts of a road, two wagon masters might hitch their teams together to pull one wagon up the slope, then leave that wagon there and go back down with the double team for the second wagon. Winters would seem to be the most difficult and dangerous time to travel. This was not always the case. A lot of extremely heavy equipment waited until winter to be moved on sleds, best pulled by the tough, long-legged mules.

Life was not easy for these animals, and one effect we don't think of today is disposing of the remains of those that did not survive. Robert Brown provides a graphic but pointed description of this problem:

> Since the nature of the San Juans frequently precluded construction of gentle grades, and since steep inclines require less time to build anyway, the lofty passes contributed materially to an incredibly high mortality rate among beasts of burden. Mules or horses that died in harness from exhaustion were often disengaged and kicked unceremoniously over the side. Far too many of these early thoroughfares were liberally endowed with decaying carcasses along the steeper grades. These circumstances gave rise to the early Colorado saying which implied that a blind man could find his way to Red Mountain Town — or whatever the community in question happened to be. The stench must have been a formidable olfactory experience indeed.[5]

Never one to let a business opportunity go by, Mears also invested in freighting from his earliest days in business, and soon his freight was traveling on the very roads which he had built. He progressed from hauling goods to meet Indian contracts in the earlier days, all the way to hauling ore from the Red Mountain Mining District down through Silverton and, until the Denver and Rio Grande (D&RG) laid rail to Silverton, on down to the D&RG line in Durango. He reminisced about packing and freighting in those early days:

> *Tens of thousands of oxen, mules, burros, and horses were required; great quantities of equipment, including heavy wagons of all kinds, lighter rigs, stage coaches, harness, pack saddles; everything that was wanted or needed had to be transferred with the aid of animals over rough roads and hazardous trails. Thousands of men and boys made their money, and some made small fortunes, in the various lines of the business of transportation, all the way from being a bull-whacker to being the owner of a line of fine stage coaches and handsome horses. Ranch men also made a fair share of money, selling hay and feed for the great numbers of animals during the winters, when the owners paid any price to prevent starvation. On first class stage routes, 20 horses were kept for each stage coach. Wherever there were people there were ten times as many head of stock (without counting cattle on the range), which meant barns, corrals, blacksmith shops, livery stables; and flies innumerable, flies everywhere.[6]*

Citizens usually called upon their county government to build public roads, but often the local governments simply didn't have enough capital. Because there was almost always money to be made in toll roads, investors were easy to find, thus providing the capital for building the roads. As seen in the example of Mears' first toll road, investors frequently had financial motivations beyond the profit gained on the tolls themselves. Often investors needed to move produce or goods for their own business interests. Tolls were charged for persons, animals, and vehicles using the road. Toll road developers usually tried to place toll stations in narrow canyons so that drivers wouldn't have the opportunity to take their wagons into the woods around the station to avoid the toll. Early toll charges ranged from one-and-a-half to fifty cents, depending on the number of people and animals and the size and weight of the load.

A list of tolls by Wooton's Ranch, which appears in the *Las Vegas Gazette* in 1865, gave the following charges:

For one wagon or carriage with one span of horses
or mules or a yoke of cattle: $1.00
One wagon or carriage with two or three spans of
mules or yokes of cattle: $1.50
One wagon or carriage with four or more spans
of horses or mules or yokes of cattle: $2.00
On horseback: $.25
Loose stock per head: $.05
Swine or sheep: $.05[7]

Roads over high mountain passes usually required higher tolls, as building such roads was, of course, more expensive. Essentially, all the tolls were set at "what the market would bear." A few years later, for example, after he had successfully completed the Ouray-Sneffels road, Mears was accused of asking exorbitant toll charges — as much as five dollars for each team and a dollar for each pack animal.[8] Mears justified his charges:

> Concerning toll charges, I had a lot of trouble. They were rated as to what the road had cost me, and also what I could get. From toll stations to cross over the mountains I charged two dollars for a single rig and for four horses it was four dollars. The highest toll was from Ouray to Silverton, a distance of twenty-six miles, for which I charged five dollars for a single span team with a fee of one dollar extra on each additional head of stock. From Ouray down the Uncompahgre Valley on the road which I bought, one dollar was charged for a single span team. The toll from the valley to Telluride was two dollars for a two-mule team.[9]

Bernice Martin reports that the toll road builders usually had a difficult time convincing the rest of the populace that their fees were either just or reasonable. There is a legend around the Saguache area concerning a situation on one of Otto Mears' early roads. It is said that an angry rancher could be heard a quarter of a mile from the toll taker he was approaching, loudly and coarsely protesting the injustice and thievery of the toll. Finally arriving at the collector's station, still angry but by now out of breath, he met a frail young man who had been listening to the tirade without a word. The young man smiled quietly, and said in a thick Russian accent, "It is enuff of the so-and-sos. Now you pay me the dollar and a half." It is further said that the cattleman handed over the money without another word.[10]

Mears' first toll road was built according to the program he generally used in all the some 450 miles of road building that eventually earned him the name, "The Pathfinder of the San Juan." First, he discovered a need to serve his own or others' business interests, and with this information, he found investors and often invested himself. He often laid out the road himself, then had the road built, and finally, used the tolls to pay off the investors and provide a profit. Robert Brown, in *An Empire of Silver*,[11] says that although Mears was not an engineer, he had a good eye for where a road could be cut, and he usually was on scene, helping direct the construction. Mears would walk and climb over the potential routes to determine the best way in which to lay his road. He often would employ capable engineers, but he usually bossed the job himself.

Later on, in and around the Red Mountain Mining District, the newspapers often reported on the dreadful conditions of Otto Mears' roads, the poor construction and the terrible maintenance — or no maintenance at all. These reports were probably true. Mears' profit-making motives would likely not encourage him to do more than the minimum necessary to provide a rough but adequate wagon way from one place to another. More than that would eat into the returns. Ken Reyher wrote:

> *Mears was so often busy building roads that he did not have time to maintain what was already built. Traffic and weather took a heavy toll, and at times some roads became next to impassable. On one occasion Mears himself came upon a wagon bogged down in deep mud near Lake City. He dutifully lent a hand and helped the two sweating and cursing teamsters get their vehicle on firmer ground, all the while listening quietly as they vented their fury toward both the road and its builder. As Mears rode away he told the pair that the man to whom they were referring would be riding*

*that same road that very day, and they would surely have
the chance to meet and converse with him. The two wagon
men, unaware who it was they were talking to, thanked
Mears profusely and the trio parted company.*[12]

Mears' first toll road, the road over Poncha Pass, was so profitable
that he soon launched into his second road-building effort by investing
in 1873 in the Saguache and San Juan Toll Road Company which was
building a road from Saguache to the mining camp of Lake City by way
of Cochetopa Pass and Los Pinos Creek. The primary investors, Isaac
Gotthelf and Enos Hotchkiss, ran into financial difficulties, and in 1874,
Mears bought out their shares in the venture. He immediately recruited
further investment to finish a rough road. It was improved in the following year, as the original road "received the excrations [sic] of nearly
every teamster who drove over it," reported the Lake City *Silver
World*. [13] At that time it was an essential link in opening Hinsdale County
and the Lake City District to miners, suppliers, and settlers.

In 1875, the citizens of Del Norte, at the southern end of the San
Luis Valley, took note of the growth of Lake City and decided to build
their own road to that town by way of Antelope Springs. At first, Mears
was against the project, fearing it would decrease business in
Saguache. The *San Juan Prospector* editorialized:

> *Evidently [Mears']* Silver World *does not want the
> road built from Antelope Springs to Lake City. We are
> assured, however, that it does not reflect the sentiments of
> the people in that vicinity so far as roads are concerned.
> The road will be built and when the travel comes by way of
> Del Norte, the* Silver World, *which has been set up to bark
> for Saguache, to sneeze when Mears takes snuff, will find
> that it has got wrong* [sic].[14]

Mears couldn't lick them, so he soon joined them, and bought a
ten per cent interest in the road from Del Norte. Enos Hotchkiss was
again hired as supervisor to "improve" this road to Lake City as he had
Mears' Saguache-to-Lake City road. It was completed in October and
became a part of the main transportation system into the San Juans.
Today's automobile travel over Slumgullion Pass on the same route
(now Colorado State Highway 149) is relatively straightforward even

with the tight curves and steep grade. In Mears' time, it was said by locals that even after Hotchkiss had improved the road, the Slumgullion Pass road should be driven only at night so that the passengers couldn't see where they had been nor where they were going.[15] Regardless of the quality of the road, however, Mears found himself in the fortunate position of owning two supply stores on the edge of the new gold and silver territory, one in Del Norte and one in Saguache. After prospectors loaded up on supplies at one of his stores, they had to pay his toll to take one of his roads into the newly developing mining area.

Ouray was a rapidly growing mining town incorporated in 1876, located some twenty-five very rough miles west of Lake City. By 1877, so many mines were being worked and the population growth was so great that Mears recognized the need for a well-equipped mercantile store in Ouray. The *Saguache Chronicle*, May 23, 1878, reported:

> *His purchases, if he made any, consisted of one of the two stocks of hardware of which the town of Del Norte boasts. Mr. Mears is now at Lake City, and we wouldn't be at all surprised to hear that he had bought the town and moved it to Ouray. That's his way of doing things.*[16]

Mears eventually built so many roads that he became known as the "Toll Road King of the San Juan." In the spring of 1878, Mears took over control of the Ouray and Lake Fork Wagon Road Company, which had been incorporated by two Ouray merchants. The toll road was originally supposed to run from Ouray to the Lake Fork of the Gunnison River and then to connect with the Saguache and San Juan Toll Road. The venture was underfinanced, and Mears bought the stock at a premium. But he decided the original plan was too ambitious, so he built the road from Ouray to a point north of the present town of Ridgway. He then formed a new toll road company, the Lake Fork and Uncompahgre Toll Road Company, to complete the route to the Saguache and San Juan Toll Road by generally following the Cimarron River and then heading east and south across Pine Creek Mesa.

After a short diversion into politics to help get his business associate Frederick W. Pitkin elected Governor of Colorado, Mears entered into his most ambitious road project to date. It ran from the terminus of the Denver & Rio Grande Railroad at the South Arkansas River across Marshall Pass to the booming area of Gunnison.

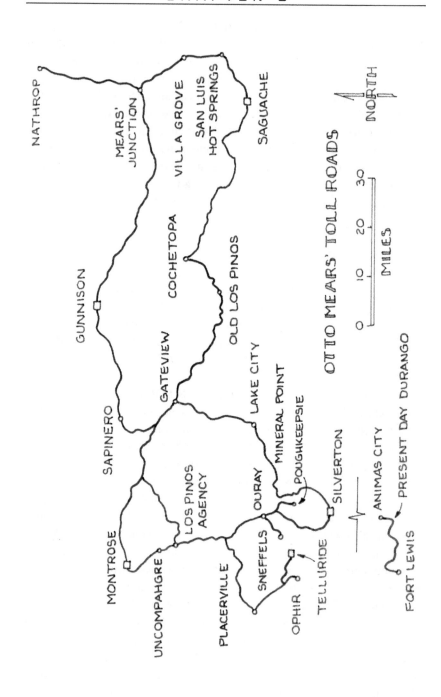

OTTO MEARS' TOLL ROADS

The Marshall Pass route had, as Marshall Sprague put it, "a rather painful history." In 1873, Lieutenant Wheeler's army surveyors were mapping out parts of the San Juan area. One of the members of the team, a Lieutenant William L. Marshall, had come down with a bad toothache. He politely declined the offer of a Silverton blacksmith to pull the tooth with horseshoe pincers and left for the nearest dentist — in Denver. His route was by way of Cinnamon Pass through Lake City. A packer named Dave Mears — no relation to Otto — traveled with him. They took three mules, two to ride and one to carry supplies.

At the foot of Cochetopa Pass, Marshall was in so much pain that he decided that there just must be a shorter and quicker trail to get to the dentist in Denver. He and his companion diverted, and by evening they had found what would be called Marshall Creek and followed it up to Marshall Pass. The next day they were able to quickly travel down Poncha Creek to Salida, and before yet another day had passed, Marshall happily submitted himself to a Denver dentist's ministration. He later stated that "his discovery of Marshall Pass was a therapeutic measure that had saved him 125 miles of trail and four days of misery."[17]

In March 1879, to take advantage of Lieutenant Marshall's fortuitous discovery, Mears, Isaac Gotthelf, and Charles Nachtrieb incorporated the Poncha, Marshall, and Gunnison Toll Road Company, which was subsidized by $25,000 in stock. Mears began construction only two weeks later and by mid-May the crew was averaging half a mile a day in new construction. Mears even brought a large herd of cattle from Oregon to feed the crew. The Marshall Pass Toll Road was well built and convenient, and it became Mears' most lucrative road-building venture. By May 1880, there was so much traffic over the road that Mears was offered $175 a day to rent the toll business to another businessman. Mears also became half owner of a coal vein five feet thick that had been uncovered in the construction. He sold the road to General Palmer and the Denver & Rio Grande Railroad in 1881 for $13,000.

There was a great deal of rivalry in the building of toll roads. When the Cottonwood Pass Toll Road was opened in mid-1880 between Buena Vista and Gunnison, an article appeared in the *Buena Vista Times:*

> *On Monday last, the work of opening the Cottonwood*
> *Pass for vehicles was finished, and now Buena Vista offers*
> *to the world the shortest and best route to the new El Dorado.*
> *. . . The route is a good mountain road, the grades not being*

as heavy as on some of the other passes, and when it is understood that by this road one goes directly to the mining regions, while, by the others many miles of travel are necessary to reach the mineral districts, after crossing the range, few will care to follow the old tedious routes by Saguache and Poncha Pass. The opening of this road will be a great boon to the miners of the Gunnison, in giving them cheaper provisions and supplies. It is unnecessary to refer to the advantages to our growing city of this new way across the continental divide. Let it be known to the miners and treasure seekers that Cottonwood Pass is open![18]

In less than a month, Mears fired a return salvo in the *Gunnison News* defending his Marshall Pass road:

There has been a great deal of adverse criticism of this route to Gunnison, the major expressions pronouncing it as a hard route and in an impassable condition. Some of this opinion comes from the ignorance of the route and the remainder to influence travel by Saguache. Having been over the route recently, we can speak advisedly of it, and qualifiedly say that it is the best, easiest and quickest route between Gunnison and railroad communication. The route has been laid out with brains, and a pass naturally hard has by skillful engineering been surmounted with a regular and easy grade, and there has been more honest work done on this road than any road we are familiar with in the State . . . . The road is in excellent condition, well bridged, free from snow and mud, and with a force of men along it to keep up its condition. It is as we stated, the shortest and best route to and from the Gunnison.[19]

Otto Mears' road building efforts were then put on hold for a while, interrupted by the Meeker Massacre and Mears' nearly full-time involvement for two years in moderating Ute Indian/Anglo relations.

In 1881 Mears formed, with Ouray merchants Charles and Ira Munn as partners, two unincorporated road building enterprises, the Dallas and San Miguel Toll Road which was to run from the town of Dallas in Ouray County to Telluride, and the San Miguel and Rico Toll

Road from Telluride on to Rico. The latter was not successful, but Mears was not deterred from investing in an incorporated toll road company, the Dallas, Parrott City, and Fort Lewis. He had purchased an old roadbed in the 1880s that he used for this project. The Denver & Rio Grande Railroad had come into Durango, and the United States Army's Fort Lewis there had received an influx of 600 troops after the Meeker Massacre. Mears saw that Durango was set to boom.

Before the Meeker Massacre, Mears had proposed a road from Gunnison to the mining community of Cebolla, but his involvement as a translator and negotiator between Colorado's Ute Indians and the United States government had prevented further activity on this project. A man named Sylvester Richardson had constructed a road along Mears' proposed route to Cebolla, but he ran into financial difficulties and sold it to Mears in 1882.

Again diverted by politics, Mears did no more road building for a year and a half. Then in August 1883, he incorporated the Ouray and Canyon Creek Toll Road Company, with $30,000 in capital, to run the ten miles from Ouray to the Mount Sneffels Mining District. The route was so rough and so precipitous that between 1876 and 1880, four different road companies had attempted but failed to construct a passable road. A fifth venture in 1880 had managed to build a road, but it was so poorly constructed that the towns of Ouray and Sneffels agreed that a better road was essential and Mears saw it as a potentially profitable venture.

When finished in 1884, the Ouray-Sneffels road was an engineering triumph. Its grade averaged three to eleven per cent, and at its steepest was "only" thirteen per cent. It was said to be one of the best built roads in the San Juans. There were soon complaints, however, about the high tolls charged, and the citizens' ire was further inflamed by Mears' scandalous lack of attention to maintenance. Before 1887 he sold the road to Ouray County for county bonds. Some say he was under considerable pressure to make the sale.

Here the story becomes murky. The local citizenry cried out that the county had paid too much for the road, and besides, the people hadn't been consulted. A judge declared that the transaction was illegal. Mears filed an appeal, which led to a second judicial decision that the sale by Mears was legal after all. As Mears himself tells the story:

In 1881, I built the line from Ouray to Sneffels, and sold it because there was a lot of fuss about the toll charge,

The rock overhang on the road from Ouray to the town of Sneffels still impresses four-wheel-drive travelers today.

*and the County of Ouray bought it from me. I had it about
a year before I sold it to the County and they gave me
County bonds. There was trouble about the bonds being
legal, and there was a trial, and I didn't bother saying anything; but a year afterwards the same lawyer was a member of the Legislature so I went and told him just what I
wanted (which was another trial without a jury), and he
said "All right." He handled it the way I wanted, and the
Judge declared the bonds were all right and legal. There
were about $7,000 for 5 miles of road; from there you can
go to Telluride, which is a short distance.*[20]

The lawyer-turned-legislator was probably a Republican, since he
was so amenable to giving Mears a hand. As will be seen in a later chapter, Mears wielded enormous power in the Colorado Republican Party.

In 1883, Mears had became intrigued by the scheme of building a
road from Ouray to the Red Mountain Mining District, a distance of about
twelve miles. Rough trails existed, but they were steep and precipitous,
and even in the best of weather were terribly treacherous to man and
pack-animal, especially on the downward trip. The existing route covered about twenty extremely rugged miles, through Poughkeepsie Gulch
and down Corkscrew Gulch. The Red Mountain District was itself at
about 11,000 feet, more than 3,000 feet altitude above Ouray. But the fab-
ulously productive Yankee Girl mine had led to a boom and rush into that
area, the largest rush since Leadville. Isolated in winter between Ouray
and Silverton, Red Mountain desperately needed good roads.

Silverton, in San Juan County, appeared to have easier access to
Red Mountain Town, although its pack trails suffered the same difficulties as those into Ouray, but Ouray leapt first into the road building
enterprise. Two failed attempts had been made to build a road. The terrain was so difficult that few investors could be found, and Ouray
County was finally forced to take over the road-building project. In 1883
the rivalry between Ouray and Silverton, especially in seeking the
wealth being hauled out of the Red Mountain Mining District, was
fierce, and advertisements, accusations, and competitive road building
plans appeared in the newspapers and in business and public offices of
both Ouray and San Juan Counties.

The Ouray County Commissioners invited Mears to look at the
work already done and to examine the records of the comatose Ouray

and San Juan Wagon Road Company to see whether he would be interested in finishing this project. In June 1883, Mears decided it would be not only possible but profitable for him to complete the road, and he agreed to do it in return for a controlling interest in the Ouray and San Juan Wagon Road Company.

This was the most difficult road building project Mears ever tackled. Even with the necessary financing, the engineering problems were staggering. The main obstacle was the Uncompahgre River Canyon. Two routes were possible — at the floor of the canyon near the river, or high above the river along the canyon wall. Below, the road would be washed away by floods; above, even if a bed could be blasted from the 800-foot quartzite walls, avalanches could sweep away the road and anything on it.

Mears, working with the county's engineers and officials, finally decided to cut a road bed into the canyon wall, some say by lowering men on ropes from the canyon rim who would use dynamite charges with fuses long enough to allow the men to be hauled up to the canyon edge before the charges were fired. It was a workable but enormously expensive solution. In the end, the toll road cost an average of nearly $10,000 per mile. Some sections of the most difficult construction partway down the quartzite cliffs cost $1000 per foot. Even with these outrageous costs, the road turned out quite profitable for Mears.

At grades of less than eleven per cent through such difficult country, the road between Ouray and Ironton, on the way to Red Mountain Town, may be the finest bit of toll road engineering ever accomplished in the United States. Nevertheless, it remained a sometimes dangerous and always difficult passage. The infamous Riverside Slide, for example, took lives until a snow shed over that part of the road was built late in the twentieth century. Lives have been lost there by avalanche as recently as 1963 when the Rev. Marvin Hudson and his daughters Amelia and Pauline were swept away in their automobile into the canyon. Even with the snow shed in place, three men lost their lives by avalanche on this highway. A stone monument stands along the road near the tribute to the Hudsons honoring those who lost their lives in the effort to keep the road open during winter's storms. On the monument are the words, "Memorial to those who have given the supreme sacrifice in the maintenance of Red Mountain Pass. The lonely vigil of the night is known only to these men of courage. Robert F. Miller, 1933-1970. Terry L. Kishbaugh, 1949-1978. Eddie J. Imel, 1953-1992." Carved into the stone is a picture of a snow-plow truck.

Today, on essentially the same bed, the "Million Dollar Highway" attracts tourists from throughout the United States and the rest of the world to gasp at its tight corners and precipitous drops, and to flinch at its absence of guardrails along some of the narrowest parts of the road and greatest heights above the river below. Many a tourist has stepped into the Ouray Visitor Center to quaver, "Is the rest of the road to Montrose . . . . like that?"

David Day, in the rather flowery style found in newspapers of the day, wrote a description of the road in the *Solid Muldoon* that is still applicable today:

> *In point of scenic grandeur the road is unequaled on the continent. Leaving the mountain clad village of Ouray, it ascends by serpentine and easy grade to a level with bluffs above town, where it winds in a southerly direction around cliffs, through wooded parks and over bridges spanning wild and romantic gulches, to Bear Creek Falls; here the route passes over the head of the roaring cataract, 253 feet above the boiling cataract below, and entering the quartzite bluffs, coils around them upon a bed of solid rock from 600 to 800 feet above the river, for a distance of two miles, when the Uncompahgre River is crossed. At this point is afforded one of the grandest views in all the land. A few hundred yards below, the waters of the Uncompahgre and Red Mountain Creek join and go roaring down a box canyon either side of which is margined with precipitous bluffs of red sandstone, dark slate and bright quartzite capped with mountains, crags and peaks of gray trachyte, reaching from their quartzite base into the land of perpetual snow.*[21]

Otto Mears briefly made some money running what he called a "hotel" at the Bear Creek Falls corner at the toll station, which itself was merely a log placed across the travel way. Even in the early days, tourists came to the area for the fantastic mountain scenery. At the toll house, travelers could stop and rest, sampling "the finest in ginger ale, pear cider, whiskeys and fine cigars, and even. . . packed lunches 'to go.'"[22]

Otto Mears' toll bridge above Bear Creek Falls, on what is now the "Million Dollar Highway." Mears' small gate-keeper's cabin huddles against the rock wall.

Long-time Ouray resident Frank Massard described the Bear Creek Falls Bridge, where the toll gate was:

Highly fanciful are the stories of the bridge over Bear Creek Falls — that it was only four feet wide — that the keeper gave the timid a shot of "Dutch Courage," and put on a blindfold before leading them across. Pure imagination! Mears built the road for wagons and the wooden bridge was the usual twelve foot width supported by "A" trusses on each side, as proven by old photographs.[23]

Mears operated the road for only eight years, when complaints about his management, principally the "exorbitant" toll rates, forced him to sell it back to Ouray County for less than it cost him to build. He tried to get the Colorado Legislature to reimburse him for his expenses, but his plea was vetoed by Governor Charles S. Thomas, apparently for political reasons.

The Silverton townspeople, in San Juan County, realized that they could not survive if all the ore mined between Silverton and Ouray was shipped out via Mears' road to Ouray. Yet they did not like the idea of hiring Mears to build a road down to Silverton, even though he had the most expertise. They objected strongly to the high tolls Mears was charging on the Ouray side of the Red Mountain District, as well as to the payment Mears was asking in public bonds and an additional "donation" from San Juan County for him to build this Red Mountain-to-Silverton road. Furthermore, Silverton citizens rightly complained that Mears would only rebuild the existing trails to make his road.

But in the end, no one else could be found to build a toll road north out of Silverton. Finally, the San Juan County Commissioners and Silverton trustees asked Mears to consider the task. He agreed, for $25,000 in Silverton municipal and San Juan County bonds and complete control of the management of the road. Much hard bargaining and considerable newspaper commentary ensued, but in the end, a written agreement was signed in 1884. The Silverton *La Plata Miner* reported that Mears also received his requested $12,000 "donation" from San Juan County.

The stipulations added to the previously agreed upon verbal contract provide an insight into the needs of roads in the area:

1. There should be a continuous down grade from the summit [of Red Mountain Pass] to Silverton.

2. The maximum grade should be not more than 350 feet to the mile. [This would provide just under a seven percent grade.]

3. There should be no curves so sharp as to prevent six animals from exerting their whole force upon the load at every point.

4. The width of the road should be such as to allow teams to pass each other at all points.

5. Ample provision should be made for drainage and for protection to winter traffic.[24]

Mears' road from Silverton to Red Mountain Town, completed in 1885, made it possible to economically freight even lower grade ore down to Silverton, and south from Silverton to Durango by rail. The combination of both roads added immeasurably to the economic growth of the Red Mountain area.

During construction of the Silverton-Red Mountain road, San Juan County asked Mears to look into building a road from Silverton north and a bit east to Mineral Point by way of Howardsville, Eureka, and Animas Forks. The old road down from Lake City over Engineer Pass was costing between $3000 and $4000 to maintain it each year. The Animas River flooded the road every spring, and the mud was a legendary consumer of wagons and loads. The mean elevation of the road would be 10,000 feet above sea level.

Mears agreed, but could not begin until completion of the Red Mountain road and the return of good weather the following spring. Meanwhile, Mears sought to increase his profits by extending the Saguache and San Juan Toll Road down the Lake Fork of the Gunnison River to the Denver & Rio Grande Railroad line on the Gunnison. He completed this Sapinero and Barnum Toll Road in the summer of 1885 and it did, indeed, prove profitable.

The most difficult part of the Silverton-Mineral Point road was between Eureka and Mineral Point. A challenging dilemma was to find a way to build up the roadbed to prevent the snow and rock slides from engulfing the road in the spring run off. But Mears and his engineers solved the problem and the road was operated profitably by Mears until 1896 when it was sold to his Silverton Northern Railroad Company for use as a railroad track and spur bed. This was the last toll road built by

Otto Mears, for as the San Juan area further developed, he turned his "pathfinding" interests from toll roads to railroads.

In less than twenty years, Mears had built a network of almost 450 miles of roads at a cost of $400,000, and made a profit in doing so. Furthermore, his road system had considerably enhanced the ability of the area to grow and prosper. Mears typically bragged, making a great deal more out of his achievements than they were perhaps worth in reality, even claiming at one point that he had done it simply to benefit the community with little thought of any profit to himself, which was obviously false. Some have said that Mears hardly made any money on his roads, but he was such a good businessman he would have had no reason to continue to build roads at a loss. Kaplan points out that in 1887, Mears still operated six toll roads, of which he owned 55.12 percent, worth $113,000. Fred Walsen, the other major stockholder, owned $86,000 worth, 41.95 percent of the stock. Kaplan has a chart of profits on the various roads that shows that Mears' net earnings over expenses on those six roads were close to thirteen percent.[25]

There has recently been some criticism of Otto Mears because he was a businessman seeking profit, rather than a humanitarian seeking to benefit his community. All of this must be considered in the context of the time in which Mears lived. As P. David Smith said, "Typical of the capitalists of his time, Mears made great personal profits from his efforts — usually at the expense of others — and although most of his gains were reinvested, it was always with the hope of making even more valuable return on his money."[26] Certainly he was a businessman, and businessmen are in the business of making money. It is indeed true that Mears used methods that were sometimes not entirely honest, did profit at the expense of others, and did cheat and lie when it seemed necessary to him. He was a hard trader and not always easy to deal with. His friend and partner John Lawrence commented once, "In the morning I, Woodson, & Fullerton went down below on horseback. We tried to settle up with Mears but as usual got mad and dident."[27] Nevertheless, Mears' efforts to make a profit did provide enormous benefit to those isolated communities and mines and other businesses of the time.

It is also true that Mears himself did not "build" or even engineer most of the roads for which he is famous. What Mears did was what any successful head of a business would do today — he had a good eye for a profitable and possible project; he hired highly skilled and creative men to design and carry out the project; he treated his workmen well and he was ahead of his time in worker relations; and perhaps most importantly, he could sell a project to investors and obtain the capital needed for these often enormously expensive ventures. Sometimes his ventures made money; sometimes they lost money. But overall, Mears' success was as an entrepreneur in the rough frontier development of the San Juan Mountains.

Otto Mears, the scrawny little man with the strong Russian accent, was also something of a visionary. Even in his old age, he foresaw the coming of the automobile and promoted improved-surface roads in Colorado. This was not popular with the taxpayers, but of course in the end, Mears was right. He also tried to get Denver to build an extensive road network with Denver in the center. In 1910 the first automobile trip was made from Del Norte to Silverton and Mears was on hand in Silverton to welcome the travelers.

That same year, the son-in-law of Mears' lifelong friend, David Frakes Day, was on the Colorado State Highway Commission. The young man visited Durango to examine a proposed improved automobile route from Denver to Durango and to seek financial contributions from the counties. At a meeting, Mears strongly supported the proposal that the Denver-Durango route be extended north to Silverton, Ouray, and the Grand Valley, helping to bring tourists to see the magnificent scenery. Mears suggested his old road beds be used for the project. Although he had sold the old Ouray and San Juan Toll Road to the County in 1891, he was on hand for the ceremony marking the beginning of the road's renovation and to provide publicity to the project.

Today's travelers along U.S. Highway 550 between Ouray and the Red Mountain Pass summit can see and experience first hand the audacity of the little man who successfully built the wagon road that would become the "Million Dollar Highway."

A family drives their buggy north on the wagon road
that will become the "Million Dollar Highway." They
carry hay in the back as fodder for the team.

CHAPTER 4

Speaking Ute with a Heavy Russian Accent

Otto Mears was economically, politically, and socially involved in the tragic conflict between the Ute Indians and the white expansionists in Colorado. His contact with the Utes began in1865, when Mears first came to the state, and ended in 1882, when he resigned as Indian Commissioner after the Utes had finally been driven from most of Colorado.

"The West" was both practically and mythically the frontier for European expansion. For the most part, except when they presented a threat, half a million Native Americans were simply ignored as unimportant to the development of the country. As a European generalization, there were only two kinds of Indians — friendly Indians and hostile Indians. The Utes of the southern Rocky Mountains, however, refused to fit into these conventional categories. They were "friendly" (that is, non-hostile) Indians who nevertheless were in the way of American expansion. The uniquely American doctrine of "manifest destiny" is exhibited here. It was the duty, even the right, of the civilized Christian European to move into the land and to "civilize," that is, to Americanize, control, or if necessary remove, whoever might already be found there.

When Mears moved his store to Conejos in 1865, Lafayette Head was the agent at the Conejos Indian Agency. Head began grooming the young Mears to eventually take over as the agent there. Mears soon managed to obtain an official contract with the United States government allowing him to trade with the Utes. Mears was to become familiar with Ute customs and was one of only a few white men ever to learn to speak the Ute language fluently, and, it is likely, was the only man ever to speak fluent Ute with a heavy Russian accent.

The Utes, pushed into the Colorado and northern New Mexico mountains by stronger tribes, were relatively secure against other Indian enemies, but not so secure against nature, especially in the harsh and bitter winters. The Utes were fortunate, however, in being one of the first Native American tribes to get horses from the Spaniards coming north out of Mexico, and the horse transformed Ute life. Their new ability to move quickly over long distances also opened new trading opportunities to the Utes with the Mexicans and with other Indian tribes. By the early 1800s, when Anglo trappers and explorers began to filter into Ute territory, the Utes totaled a few thousand members.

The encroaching Americans made three major treaties with the Utes — in 1863, 1868, and the Brunot Treaty of 1873. D.C. Oakes was the interpreter for the 1868 treaty, and Otto Mears for the treaty negotiations in 1873. There were three main problems with these treaties. In the first place, the American government insisted on treating "the Utes" as a single entity, demanding that they present a single leader to interface with Washington. This was contrary to the reality of Ute social organization into seven loosely associated bands. Second, the basic intent of the United States government was to force the Utes to be something that they were not — to turn them from their gathering and hunting and nomadic life into settled farmers. Agriculture was a way of life that the Utes considered degrading and shameful. The third and certainly the most egregious problem was that the United States kept breaking the treaties that it did manage to make with the Utes by not following through on its own promises. This is not to say that all fault was on the side of the Americans, but it was the Americans who were trying to force the Utes and not the other way around. American expansionism fueled the entire process, and it was Anglo-European racism that was all too often a silent motivator behind American-Indian interactions.

By 1865, the United States government was trying to get the Utes to settle on reservations and stay in one place. Because the Utes had survived by a nomadic life of gathering and hunting, the government promised to make up the difference by providing goods and animals. In 1865, for example, soon after he arrived near Conejos, Colorado, Otto Mears gained a contract to sell to the Ute Indian Agency these supplies for the Indians. Too often the United States failed to provide the promised supplies because of cheating, theft, loss, misappropriation, and, especially during the Civil War, simple preoccupation with other priorities. The minds of Washington politicians and political priorities were a long way away from the Rocky Mountain West.

The treaty of 1868, known as the Hunt Treaty, reaffirmed the agreements and boundaries of the 1863 treaty. The Utes were given the land composing much of the Western Slope of Colorado to keep "forever." No white person was to pass through or reside on this land. The boundaries of this land, which was reserved in perpetuity for the Utes, were, on the

West, the present Utah border; to the East, the 107th meridian (approximately two miles west of present Gunnison); to the South, the present New Mexico border; and to the North, the northern edge of present-day Rio Blanco County, Colorado. There was one exception held by the Americans — that roads, highways, and railroads might cross Ute territory as authorized by law. Even at the beginning, the Utes pointed out that having the Indian agents and their families living at the Los Pinos Indian Agency on the Ute reservation broke the treaty — but to no avail.

But of course the Americans had not yet discovered gold and silver in the San Juan Mountains. That discovery added a forceful new factor into the situation. In spite of Ute violence and American military policing efforts, the prospectors kept coming. In 1869 the American government determined to create a new agency at Los Pinos and to establish the Los Pinos Ute Indian Reservation. Otto Mears was given a contract by the government to build a road from Saguache to the new Los Pinos Agency to bring in the promised supplies, many provided by Mears, for distribution to the Utes.

There is a much-repeated story concerning Mears' cheating the government — and the Utes — in a transaction involving cattle transferred to the agency. The accusation was made in a letter from the new Indian Agent, Lieutenant Calvin Speer, to Superintendent of Indian Affairs, and later Territorial Governor, General Edward McCook. Speer stated that "Mr. Mears also advised Mr. Russell to leave out Fifty Cows and not brand them. . . he had some old hides that he would brand and then say the cows had died. Thereby making Fifty-Cows, and he would make it all right with Speer . . . ."[1] However, in the same letter Speer accused Mears of being a Democrat.[2] Speer's latter accusation is obviously nonsense as Mears was even then something of a power in the Republican Party in Colorado. A witness so unreliable as to accuse Mears of being a Democrat can be given little credence regarding the story of the fifty cow hides. This is not to say that Mears didn't ever connive or cheat, but this particular story, though often repeated, is questionable. At any rate, Mears continued with his contracts to supply the agency with cattle in addition to such goods as flour, hay, potatoes, oats, and beans. Bernice Martin describes their distribution:

When the Utes, as many as 2000 at some times, received their distribution at the Agency, distributions of live cattle were made to the elders. The Indians made quite a production of the distribution of the beef on the hoof. One beef cow was allotted to the head of each family. Stripping down for action, he mounted his horse, took up his rifle, and waited outside the corral. Then the gates were opened and the cattle booed out of the corral while the Indians yelled and howled until the frightened animals scattered in all directions. When the cattle had a good head start, the braves pursued, riding with a reckless abandon which often resulted in tumbles and broken bones, shouting the cattle down as if they were the buffalo the Utes liked to hunt on the plains.[3]

In what we today would consider a strange arrangement, different churches were assigned responsibility for the various Indian agencies, and the Los Pinos Agency was under the care of the Unitarians. Therefore, in 1871, Speer, a Catholic, was abruptly dismissed and the Unitarian church appointed Jabez Nelson Trask to take his place, although it took Trask a year and a half to get to Colorado. He was a Harvard educated man dreadfully ignorant of the Indians and the frontier. He aroused Ute antagonism from the very beginning.

The Utes eventually forced the United States to remove Trask from the post at which he had done a miserable job. The Utes wanted the United States to appoint Army Colonel Albert Pfeiffer, former Indian Agent at Taos, and an adopted brother to the Utes. Governor McCook however appointed "General" Charles Adams. (He held the rank of General only through brief service in the Territorial Militia.) Even though he was a brother-in-law of McCook's, the Utes found him acceptable, and history shows he did a reputable job. McCook, by the way, continued to take care of his relatives by appointing his wife's brother, James B. Thompson, as Superintendent of Indian Affairs.

Charles Marsh states that General Adams and his wife did a creditable job at the agency, and led the effort to meet the American obligations in accordance with terms of the 1868 treaty. Marsh also provides an otherwise unrecognized career to Otto Mears — fur trapper — stating that "Supplies of blankets, utensils, and food were laboriously hauled by wagon to the Los Pinos Agency by a former fur trapper and trader, Otto Mears, under contract with the government."[4]

Governor McCook had always wanted the Utes out of Colorado, and many other whites felt the same way. There was a general feeling among the Americans that the Utes weren't "using" the land and therefore didn't deserve to hold it. By "using," the whites generally meant "exploiting" for agriculture, ranching, or mining. It is an attitude we don't fully understand in these days of natural ecology and cultural preservation. An item from the *Boulder News* expresses the attitude of that time: "The Los Pinos Indian Council has failed in its object. The Utes would not resign their reservation, so the fairest portion of Colorado and some of the richest mining country is closed by force of arms. So settled we believe it will be and should be. An Indian has no more right to stand in the way of civilization and progress than a wolf or a bear."[5]

The Utes stood on their rights by treaty, but the prospectors, miners, and investors continued to put pressure on the United States government. One of those prospectors was Frederick W. Pitkin, a wealthy mining investor who ardently wanted to add the San Juans to Colorado Territory. Pitkin later used his power and Otto Mears' growing influence in the Republican Party to become the second governor of the State of Colorado in 1880.

In early 1872 a meeting was held with a Congressionally appointed team consisting of Territorial Governor McCook, John D. Lang (a member of the U.S. Board of Indian Commissioners), and General John McDonald. Indian Agent Charles Adams brought Chief Ouray, two other Utes, and Otto Mears as interpreter to Denver for preliminary meetings.

For the official meeting with the Utes at the Agency the following August, McCook invited Felix Brunot, a Pittsburgh steel magnate and organizer of the American Church Missionary Society, to attend. A great many speeches were made by the Americans, but the Utes heard no good reason to give up their lands, and no agreement was made. As P. David Smith points out in his biography of Chief Ouray, "The white man couldn't figure out what to do. The Utes were friendly Indians. If they had been hostile, their land would have been taken by force, but the Utes had even been allies with the United States in its wars against hostile Indian tribes."[6] Chief Ouray himself put it: "The Army conquered the Sioux. You can order them around. But we Utes have never disturbed you whites. So you must wait until we come to your ways of doing things."[7] Mears suggested to Brunot that since the problem was that Ouray did not trust the McCook Commission, Brunot should come back alone the following year to continue negotiations.[8]

Prospectors and settlers continued to clamor for Ute cession of the San Juans. Brunot did return the following August. This time, John Lawrence acted as interpreter, but again negotiations broke down.

Bernice Martin says that, "Felix Brunot, as the Chairman of the Board of Indian Commissioners, represented American idealism at its best, but he was continually hamstrung by the machinations of the corrupt and dishonest politicians who surrounded him, in particular the shabby opportunism of Colorado's Governor McCook."[9] Brunot turned to Otto Mears for advice. Mears suggested that Chief Ouray should receive a salary of $1,000 each year for the next ten years. Brunot said that he felt that the government had no business offering a bribe, but Mears insisted that this would not be a "bribe" but a salary, so that the Chief would have a dignified way of making his living.

Brunot extended this offer to Ouray, and additionally he proposed that the Utes receive the annual interest on $500,000. In return, the Utes would give up four million acres in the San Juans, keeping a remaining fourteen million acres upon which they could live in peace. The Utes agreed to this treaty, influenced by the leadership of Ouray who seemed to realize that the whites were going to have the San Juans one way or another, and he would do well for his people to negotiate the best deal he could. Otto Mears had spoken with Ouray in lengthy meetings to try to explain the inability of the government to control the migration of men to the San Juan mining camps. Mears said, "It is much better sometimes to do what does not please us now, if it will be best for our children later."[10] Brunot had told Ouray frankly that if the government attempted to force the miners out, this would bring on a war, and the Utes would lose their land without receiving any recompense.[11] The Utes surrendered the area of what are now the counties of Dolores, La Plata, Hinsdale, Ouray, San Juan, Montezuma, and San Miguel. Brunot was exultant that the treaty had been signed. The Utes ended up receiving only twelve cents an acre, at a time when the United States Government was charging $1.25 per acre for far less valuable homestead land in the West.

After the signing of the treaty, Brunot recommended to his superiors that a one-month, expense-paid trip to Washington be arranged for Ouray and the other nine important Ute Chiefs. Otto Mears, General Charles Adams, and his assistant Herman Lueders were to accompany them as guardians and guides. The plan was not entirely altruistic. The government intended to impress upon the Ute Chiefs the gravity and importance of this treaty.

Traveling by train, the group arrived in Washington in October, where they visited the sights around the capital city until they could meet with the Secretary of Indian Affairs and the Secretary of the Interior to discuss final details of the Brunot Treaty. The Utes were given tours of the Treasury Department and the naval yard, and a ride on a warship. The Utes were even taken to the White House to meet President and Mrs. Grant. The Ute Chiefs were traveled through Boston, Philadelphia, New York, Chicago, and St. Louis. On a lighter note, Mears took the Utes to a circus, a play, art galleries, and the zoo in New York's Central Park. The entire trip was calculated to give them an impression of the vast power of the white man and the solemnity and inviolability of the Treaty. One wonders what might have been done to impress the United States similarly, as the Americans proceeded to break this "inviolable" treaty within less than a decade.

The *Chicago Tribune's* "Washington Special" dated October 17, 1873, commented:

> *The delegation of Ute Indians that visited Washington left for their Reservation today. They will take back with them greater feelings of disgust than they brought East; this tribe has ceded to the Government four million acres of mining country for which they are to receive an annual annuity of $25,000, which annuity would be the accrued interest on $500,000 which the Government owes them for the relinquishment of what is known as the San Juan Mining Region. On the even of their departure they held a final interview with the commissioner of Indian Affairs who "impressed" on them the necessity of vacating their old haunts immediately and of removing to their new Agency on the Uncompahgre. Mr. Mears acted as interpreter on their last interview. The Ute chiefs, with the exception of Ouray, who was visiting at the home of Colorado's Representative, stoutly contended that the annuity of $25,000 a year annually forever which they were to receive from the Government was to be spent as the Indians pleased, but they were "impressed" to believe that they would have to allow their money to be spent for them, as their agents and Government might deem best.* [12]

The federal government began spending the Utes' money for them immediately and continued to do so. Ute "earnings" on the $500,000 held by the United States were used to meet the expenses of the Indian agencies and to supply the material needs of the Utes for cattle and grain, needs caused by the Americans' taking their hunting land in the first place and forcing the Utes onto reservations. The *Pueblo Tribune* reported of the 1880 trip by Ouray, Chipeta, and others to Washington, that the expenses of the Utes' trip to Washington would be borne, not by the taxpayers, but would come from the interest payments to the Utes from the federal government, funding called the "San Juan Purchase."[13]

Mears tells the story of a trip he and Mary made to visit Chief Ouray after the Agency was moved to the Uncompahgre River area in 1875:

> *I made the trip to the Uncompahgre Agency, where the city of Montrose now stands. Ouray was head chief then and I wanted to see him. The distance was 150 miles, and I went by buggy with my wife and baby. When we were nearly at the place, we found that the river was badly flooded and we could not ford it. We had to get across for we could not stay where we were. Finally I thought of a plan. I had two empty oat sacks, for of course we had to carry all our provisions and fodder for the horses with us. I filled these sacks with rocks and tied one on each end of the back axle, and I drove my rig full speed.*
>
> *The horses swam, dragging the buggy after them. The buggy could not upset, because the two loaded sacks held it down, just as two anchors would. The water rose as we sat in the buggy. My wife held the baby up in her arms. I tried to guide the ponies. When we reached the other side I heard the firing of guns and an Indian ran past me. Ouray came out and called me to come into the house as quickly as I could. He lived in a "doby" house and after we went in he barred the doors and windows. He said that the Indian we had seen had been sent out by the Northern Utes to try to induce his Indians to rebel and join with them in an insurrection against Ouray as Chief.*
>
> *When Ouray heard this he ordered the Indian shot. He told us that there would be trouble during the night. We did not sleep much, but kept on the lookout as Ouray felt that the Northern Utes would come down on him. We were not par-*

Chief Ouray of the Tabeguache Utes together with part-time United States Indian Commissioner and English-Ute translator Otto Mears.

ticularly comfortable in between these two fires, the Northern Utes on the one hand and Ouray with his Indians on the other.

The next morning, all being quiet, I hitched up and drove on to the government agency ten miles away. On the road we passed the dead body of the Indian we had seen shot the night before. We stayed at the agency ten days and when we came back, the body still lay as we had seen it. It was badly decayed and covered with buzzards, who were eating the flesh, but not one of Ouray's Indians could be induced to bury it.[14]

Mears continued his close ties with the Utes until the Meeker Massacre in 1879. Because of his abilities with the Ute language and the apparent respect the Utes had for him, he also remained an unofficial advisor on their concerns. Mears made sure he took financial advantage of the situation. He did what he could to ensure that as the Utes became more dependent on United States government supplies, Mears himself held contracts to provide those supplies. In addition to beef and grain, Mears now contracted to supply items such as soda, soap, salt, dry goods, and hardware.

Tensions continued to rise between the invading Americans and the beleaguered Ute Indians. In the spring of 1878, a new agent reported for duty at the White River Agency. His name was Nathan C. Meeker, one of the organizers of the Utopian colony at Greeley. He was a missionary at heart and believed that it was his duty to "elevate and enlighten" the Utes. Among the nicer things he has been called are "humorless" and "overbearing." He was determined to build an agricultural colony and "civilize" the Utes into becoming farmers upon it. Meeker found that he could interact fairly well with Douglas, an older leader of the Yampa Utes, but most of the younger Utes were following a younger man, Nicaagat or "Jack."

While Nicaagat was away, Meeker moved the White River Agency about fifteen miles downriver to a better agricultural site. When Nicaagat returned, Meeker ordered him and his group to move to the new site as well. Nicaagat refused.

By early 1879, Meeker had some buildings under construction and forty acres of land plowed, almost all the work having been done by white employees. The Utes demanded they be paid for labor as well, which Meeker did under protest until his funds ran out.

"The *Ouray Times*, December 1877, was asking why 'non-producing, semi-barbarous' people occupied land which 'intelligent and industrious citizens' could use."[15] Meeker much valued having his ideas in print. He published an article, similarly slanted as the quote above, in the *Greeley Tribune*, where his ideas were picked up by Frederick Pitkin, Otto Mears' political crony, and William B. Vickers, a virulently anti-Indian editor and politician in Denver. Vickers wrote an article for the *Denver Tribune* that was reprinted across Colorado under the banner, "The Utes Must Go!"

The White River Utes learned that the letter of their agent, Meeker, helped to fuel the Ute-removal movement, and that Meeker wrote that the Utes' land did not belong to them but to the government, which was "loaning" it to them. Vickers manufactured rumors about Ute crime and Governor Pitkin demanded the Utes be kept on their reservation. Nicaagat appealed in person to Pitkin for a replacement for Meeker, but of course to no avail.

Conditions continued to deteriorate through a number of incidents, until the War Department ordered Major Thomas Thornburgh to march to the White River Agency. At Milk River, the troops and the Utes came to battle. Later, the whites blamed the Utes, and the Utes the whites. It appears the actual shooting started with a single shot. No one knows for sure which side fired it, but it was most likely the Utes. When the Utes near the Agency heard about the battle, a dozen of them took their rifles to the agency and shot every white man in sight, including Meeker, and then mutilated the body of the hated agent. They captured the three white women and two children at the agency and fled with their captives toward an old Ute camp on Piceance Creek.

The fighting continued at Milk River for almost a week. During the first night, a scout, Joe Rankin, managed to escape and ride 160 miles in twenty-eight hours to get reinforcements sent from Wyoming. Major Thornburgh was killed in the first skirmish. The Army lost twelve killed, forty-three wounded; and the Utes lost thirty-seven of some three hundred warriors.

As soon as Ouray heard about the conflict, he sent a message by runner to the Utes to stop the fighting. At the same time, cavalry reinforcements arrived for the whites. The White River Utes surrendered their captives. The women at first said they had not been abused, but later said that they had been. The first story may have been told out of Victorian shyness or perhaps there was no abuse. The second version could have been true, or could have been invented later to support the movement to move the Utes out of Colorado.

In any case, it was too late to save the Utes' claim to western Colorado. Even though an elderly and sick Ouray traveled with Otto Mears (newly appointed an Indian Commissioner), Shavano, and Ouray's wife Chipeta to Washington to plead for the Utes, the Utes were nonetheless ousted from Colorado and sent to live in Utah on land that even the Mormons did not want. Today, few realize the anger and hatred many whites had against the Indians, especially after the Meeker Massacre. When the Ute representatives traveled to Washington in 1880 they were very nearly attacked and even lynched on the way, as reported in the *Pueblo Tribune:*

> *Chief Ouray, Chipeta his squaw, and the other ten Washington bound Utes, left Alamosa yesterday morning for the East, a small escort of soldiers accompanying them as far as Larkin, Kansas . . . . Otto Mears, formerly post-trader at Los Pinos Agency, will go with the party, by request of Ouray . . . . A car is reserved for the Utes by each of the [rail] roads, and no one except those who compose their escort is admitted. This arrangement created much dissatisfaction among the eager crowds who gathered on the platform at every station along the Denver & Rio Grande, but subsequent events proved [it] to be a wise plan, so far as securing the safety of the Indians was concerned. As the train rolled out of Alamosa, the body of the Mexican lynched that morning came into view, and the red skins gazing from the car windows were appalled at the spectacle, not recovering their usual equanimity for several hours. Chipeta was so shocked as to shed tears, and for some time was not coaxed into her usual cheerfulness and good humor. No doubt the Utes thought that their chance of going through the state unharmed, which hanged men for stealing, was very small, and their reception at Pueblo did very little towards reassuring them.*
>
> *The depot at that place was crowded when the train stopped, there being hardly enough room on the platform for another person. Nearly two thousand people were present and the air was rent with shouts of threatening import to the Utes. Lieutenant Taylor, commanding the military escort, formed the Utes in single file, each one between two soldiers, and marched them aboard the Atchison, Topeka & Santa Fe train . . . . . In spite of these precautions some of the Indians were struck by pieces of coal thrown at them from a distance, and others received blows from the fists of some persons in the crowd as they ascended the steps of the car.*
>
> *After the trembling reds had been safely bestowed in the eastward bound cars The Tribune reporter heard the following [from a citizen of Pueblo]: "If we wanted to do it*

we could raise a crowd of a hundred men to take these red devils from you and lynch them." [16]

Lynching was not an idle threat. The *Pueblo Tribune*, in a dispatch regarding the same incident, reported that five hundred men could easily have been aroused to attack the Ute party. Fortunately, cooler heads prevailed, and the Indians were allowed to pass without more violence. [17]

Seven of the eight Ute leaders signing the 1880 treaty made their "X"; Ouray signed his name. Otto Mears, Interpreter, was listed as a witness. Chief Ouray died on August 24, 1880. Very few of the Utes had signed the new treaty, and it required three-fourths approval to ratify it. At this time, Otto Mears traveled Ute territory, paying two dollars out of his own pocket to every Ute who would sign the agreement. Even so, some say he actually only obtained 110 signatures. [18] Somehow, out of more than 3000 tribal members, this was accounted by the authorities as the three-fourths approval they needed.

Bribery charges against Mears were filed by Indian Commissioners Manypenny and Meacham to Secretary of the Interior Carl Schurz. Mears filed his response to Schurz, but before Schurz could follow up on it, James A. Garfield was elected President and Schurz was replaced by Samuel J. Kirkwood. Nevertheless, Mears was ordered to Washington to stand trial on bribery charges before Secretary Kirkwood. Mears' defense involved his description of the powder-keg situation in Colorado at the time and the complication of Ouray's death. He agreed that in order to convince the White River and Uncompahgre Utes to move, he had paid them two dollars apiece. Mears claimed that the Utes felt that two dollars in cash was worth more to them than the government's promise of fifty thousand dollars a year in the future, which they would probably never get.

> *'Was the money you paid them your own, or was it paid by the government?' Kirkwood asked. 'I paid it out of my own pocket,' Mears replied. 'How much did it cost you?' Kirkwood asked. 'Twenty-eight hundred dollars,' replied Mears. 'Send me a bill for it,' Kirkwood said, 'and I will see to it that the government reimburses you. You did a good job and I am grateful,' Kirkwood continued. I know a little about Indian character too, and I think that you were perfectly right in handling this matter as you did. Can you*

remove the Utes as the treaty specifies?' Mears replied,
'Yes, if you give me enough troops and keep Manypenny
and Meacham out of the way.'[19]

After Mears returned from Washington, Meacham and Manypenny again opposed him regarding just where the new reservation boundaries should be set. Mears argued that the treaty gave the United States the right to move the Utes all the way to Utah rather than just to the Grand Valley in Colorado. The precise wording in the treaty was, "The Uncompahgre Utes agree to remove and settle upon agricultural lands on the Grand River near the mouth of the Gunnison River in Colorado, if a sufficient quantity of agricultural land shall be found there; if not, then upon such other unoccupied agricultural lands as may be found in that vicinity and in the Territory of Utah."[20] Later, Mears said that he had pushed for moving the Utes to Utah because he knew the whites would sooner or later want the fertile Grand Valley land, and he wanted to forestall yet another confrontation with the Utes. Mears also contracted to provide supplies to the new agency and construct the agency buildings in Utah. Although it might be claimed that Mears was taking advantage of the Utes, in fact, he was heavily criticized by the whites as pro-Indian.

Sidney Jocknick relays a much-repeated story that Mears was one of two Indian Commissioners who signed the order to finally move the northern Utes out of Colorado. "That night at 2 o'clock, General MacKenzie sent for Mr. Mears and Judge McMorris, who were the only commissioners present at the time, and told them if they would sign the order to remove the Indians he would do so with his troops."[21]

That story has been repeated by many over the last century, but in 1975, James G. Schneider refuted the accusation against Mears:

The frequent repetition of this story has led to Mears'
being cast as "the heavy" in this drama. It has appeared
that he, practically single-handedly, forced the Utes out of
Colorado. But such was not the case! There is no doubt that
Otto and all of the Commissioners, Agent Berry and
Secretary Kirkwood had agreed that the Utes would be
required to move to the new location in Utah, but the actual
*request for MacKenzie to use force if necessary was **not***
given by Otto Mears. It was given by Judge McMorris, who
*was the **only** Commissioner present at the Uncompahgre*

at that time. The records of the Commission conclusively prove this, and further show that Mears was in Utah at the time, in charge of erecting the buildings for the new Agency. Thus another apocryphal story bites the dust.[22]

The removal of the Utes could not be done without preparation. Mears went to Salt Lake City to help arrange for accommodations and provisions to be ready for the Uncompahgre and White River Utes when they arrived in Utah. Government surveys also had to be made to establish boundary lines and roads and bridges had to be constructed to enable the movement of the groups of people and their livestock.

In September 1881, the last group of Utes made its exodus from western Colorado. General John Pope wrote that the whites who gathered in view of the Ute river crossing were so eager and unrestrained that military force was required to keep the whites off the reservation until the Utes had left.[23] General MacKenzie protected the Utes with his troops against the angry and eager whites, and did all he could to assist them in their departure. He had large boats brought to the crossings of the Grand and Green Rivers, and used them to ferry the Indians across, along with their possessions and livestock. The "MacKenzie boats" remained there for many years and were used as ferries by western immigrants.

A story in the *Pueblo Chieftain* relates that even in all this difficulty, Mears managed to make a profit:

> *The story is told that while General MacKenzie's soldiers were escorting Indians out of Western Colorado over Mears' Ouray Toll Road, Mears demanded the usual fee for use of this road. The General told Mears that unless he opened the gates for free passage he would have his men tear them down.*
>
> *"You do it and it will cost you your commission," Mears told the General. Knowing that Mears carried weight in Washington, the General reluctantly signed vouchers for use of the wagon road. It has been estimated that the General authorized about $100,000 for the right to use the road during the campaign.*[24]

Shortly after the Utes' arrival in Utah, Mears, in his capacity as an Indian Commissioner, made an inspection trip to make sure of the sufficiency of shelter and supplies. It was reported back in Colorado that Cojoe, a Ute chief, tried to kill Mears, claiming that Mears was largely responsible for the Uncompahgre band's having to leave Colorado. Over the next year and a half, there were other attempts on Mears' life. He resigned as a commissioner in April 1882. The commission itself was abolished in 1883.

As Kaplan points out in *Otto Mears: Paradoxical Pathfinder*, Otto Mears did use bribery, coercion, and manipulation to help push so many Ute Indians out of Colorado, but Kaplan also points out that much can be said in his favor considering the facts of the potentially explosive situation. Mears had considerable diplomatic skills and political contacts, which he used to the fullest to do what he believed best. As always with Otto Mears, his actions were not purely altruistic:

> *His actions as Indian Commissioner not only contributed to Colorado's growth but proved personally profitable as well . . . . He was paid well as a commissioner, and in addition, he augmented his salary by fulfilling contracts to build and supply the new reservation at Green River.*[25]

Even today, the controversy roils about the treatment of the Utes in Colorado and Mears' role in that series of events. Sometimes we tend to forget that most people, even unusually successful or famous ones, are of their own times. Otto Mears has been strongly criticized not least for his behavior toward the Utes. Only recently, columnist Bob Ewegen of the *Denver Post* took Mears to task for his actions in the Ute removal from Colorado. In a column from the *Denver Post* of Monday, July 14, 1997, Ewegen wrote in a column entitled "Two Bucks for a Birthright:"

> *There's a stained glass window in the Colorado Senate honoring Otto Mears as 'The Pathfinder.'*
> *My wife would offer a blunter title for Mears: 'The Scoundrel.'*
> *"My wife, novelist Yvonne Montgomery, is part Cherokee and thus sympathizes with the Utes who once owned almost of all of Colorado's Western" land.*[26]

Ewegen quotes Gladys R. Bueler's *Colorado's Colorful Characters:*

> *"The Utes, for whom the San Juans had been home for generations, naturally resented the rush of white men to*

lands they considered their own. Otto Mears made remov-
ing the Indians to smaller reservations to the west his first
order of business, thereby opening this area of settlement.
He played a prominent role in drawing up the various
treaties by which the Utes lost their lands. The first was the
Brunot Treaty of 1873 . . . in which the Utes gave up their
San Juan area for a payment of $25,000 a year.

". . . In 1880 Mears was asked to serve as one of the
five commissioners to make another treaty with the Utes.
The government was prepared to pay $1.8 million to the
Indians for the balance of their land, 11 million acres on
the Western Slope. Mears had a better idea. He gave each
Indian $2 to sign the treaty, thereby saving the govern-
ment practically the total sum it had expected to pay." [27]

As noted above, Mears' offering of the two dollars per signature to the Utes saved the government nothing, but it may have saved a brutal war with the Utes. Ute removal, though unfair, may have saved lives in the long run, as the American prospectors and developers were determined to have the land for their own use.

At the time, white businessmen and government officials thought it a good thing to move the Indians out of Colorado. The Dawson Scrapbooks contain a commendation to Otto Mears, giving him the "credit" for driving the Indians out of Colorado.[28] As late as 1958, Mears was posthumously given a First Citizen, "Civis Princeps" award from Regis College. A number of awards were given in agriculture, architecture, commerce, fine arts, and so on. The category of Mears' award? Government — for his "negotiations with Indians that resulted in acquisition of the territory that now embraces Grand Junction, Montrose, and Delta" as well as for his service in the Colorado legislature.[29]

As always with Otto Mears, one cannot declare him either a hero or a villain, but like so many successful men, he is a complex mixture of self-advancement and service to his community. It is easy to look back and criticize Mears' attitudes about and actions toward the Indians. Given the high feelings against the Utes at the time, however, by ensuring the Utes' removal from most of the state of Colorado, Mears may indeed have saved them from even more hardship and death. It is possible that if Mears had used his influence in 1873 to arrange a treaty that put the Utes in Utah at that time, the Meeker

Massacre might have been avoided. Without such an event as the Meeker Massacre, however, it is unlikely that the whites would have had strong enough motivation to force the Utes' removal.

In the end, the Ute territory was reduced from an area extending from present-day Denver to Salt Lake City, and from Wyoming into New Mexico, to three reservations — the smallest, the Southern Ute Reservation in southwestern Colorado; the Ute Mountain Reservation around the four-corners area and including land in southeastern Utah, southwestern Colorado, and a small piece in New Mexico; and the extensive Uintah and Ouray Reservation in northeastern Utah. Otto Mears made his mark on a people, for well or for ill.

CHAPTER 5

Joker in the Republican Deck

Otto Mears was involved in politics from his earliest days in Colorado. As soon as he and John Lawrence successfully lobbied to get Saguache County created, Mears was appointed County Treasurer. He was subsequently elected and served three terms in that office. Throughout the rest of his life, Mears participated, sometimes intensely, in politics but he never isolated his political activities from his business activities. Rather than the lust for power, of which he has been accused, Mears' life-long intent was primarily to make money. Politics was a means to that end, just as his work with the Utes did not hinder, but in fact helped, his business interests. Mears became quite a force in the Republican Party in Colorado from its earliest days.

Mears played what we could call "dirty politics," though his actions were perhaps no more corrupt than those of most politicians of the time. His political machinations clearly show Mears to be more complex than just a "hero" or "pathfinder." "Scoundrel" and "manipulator" are other terms that apply equally well. To see a rounded picture of Otto Mears, we must take his political activity into account.

John Lawrence, a staunch Democrat, reports in his diary on early days in Saguache politics:

> *August 28, 1870. As the people were all working on the cut-off road between here & the Agency yesterday we did not hold our preliminary meeting in this precinct to elect deligates to the convention to be held on the 30th, but quite a large number of people met here this morning and Fullerton, F. Chaves & myself were elected. . . .*
>
> *August 30, 1870 . . . I & our deligation went down to the general convention where we nominated Woodson for County Commissioner, Chas. Baldwin for county clerk, Isaac Gotthelf for county treasurer, James Fullerton for Sheriff, John Lawrence for Assessor, and James Downer*

for school superintendent. Mears got hostile because we did not nominate him for treasurer.

> *September 1, 1870 . . . there was a Republican convention at Mearses. They nominated . . . Mears for treasurer and Godfrey for School Superintendent.*[1]

Bernice Martin, Lawrence's editor, reports: "Lawrence's ticket was elected with the exception that Otto Mears was reelected treasurer. The feuding between the two men was short-lived apparently, because they were working as partners in a number of projects in the weeks ahead."[2]

Another example of Mears' and Lawrence's political differences is the story of the vote buying scheme to make Saguache the county seat, when Mears and Lawrence mutually indicted each other regarding buying and selling votes.

In 1870, Mears was the Republican representative from Saguache County to the Territorial Convention. Only a few years later, he was his county's representative on the Republican State Central Committee. By the time Colorado gained statehood in 1876, Mears was a deeply involved political power in the Republican Party.

There was not a great deal of difference between the Colorado political parties of the time, according to *A Colorado History:*

> *Actually, the parties seldom seriously differed in outlook, nor did any permanent issues sharply divide them. Both Republicans and Democrats tended toward conservatism; both seemed more interested in offices and the resulting spoils than in any major reform issues (in this way they were not much different from their counterparts on the national scene). Nominations and elections often pivoted on personalities and money, and often degenerated into name-calling and personal slander.*[3]

Mears probably chose to be a Republican because he saw greater opportunity there, not for any strong belief in the platform of one party over the other.

In 1876, Mears traveled to Pueblo as a delegate to the Republican Convention from Saguache County, where he was immediately appointed to serve on the Convention's committee for permanent organization. He also participated in the selection of the party's slate for the first state election — John L. Routt for governor and Lafayette Head for Lieutenant Governor. It is likely that Mears had a good deal to do with Head's nomination, as they were former business partners and friends. Mears liked to nominate men with whom he was familiar, and especially those with whom he could negotiate political favors. It was said generally by the populace and in newspapers that he never helped elect anyone without coming to the elected official afterward for some kind of payoff. The Republican Party slate won the election for the top offices in the newly created State of Colorado.

That November, Mears was chosen as one of three presidential electors from Colorado by a joint session of the legislature. Mears became the messenger to carry Colorado's three electoral votes for Rutherford B. Hayes to Washington.

In the summer of 1878, the Republican State Convention nominated Frederick Pitkin to run for governor. Mears was a prime mover in this nomination. Pitkin ran, and he won. But Pitkin made the mistake afterward of not paying his political debts, ignoring his home county of Ouray, and failing to promote the interests of those who had put him in his position.[4] That unhealthy activity soon ensured Pitkin's political death in the Republican Party of Colorado.

Political life is an expensive business, and the early history of the State of Colorado presented no exception. Otto Mears had not only benefited financially by his assignment as an Indian Commissioner, but that work gave him front-page exposure in every Colorado newspaper. The publicity, even when it was negative, was invaluable. Rather than being one of several State Republican Party bosses, Otto Mears became a familiar name everywhere. He was so well placed that he was able to claim with some truth that no U. S. Senator from Colorado or governor of the state could be elected without his favor.[5]

In 1881, Mears won his party's nomination to the legislature and his election came in a bitterly contested campaign based more on the disagreements between Mears' supporters on the one hand and his enemies on the other than on party politics. During much of 1882 and 1883, he therefore devoted his political energy to his role as a state legislator representing Saguache County in the Fourth General Assembly. One of the major activities of his term involved the creation of new counties in the territory that had been vacated by the Utes. If history had gone only a little differently, western Colorado would have ended up with a "Mears" County instead of a Montrose County.

At that time, one of the duties of any state legislature was to select the state's representatives to the United States Senate. In 1883 it was necessary to elect both a long-term and a short-term senator, the latter because President Chester A. Arthur had appointed former Colorado Senator Teller to his Cabinet. Contention for the appointments to the United States Senate seats was great. Mears had run for the state legislature on his promise to vote for Pitkin for U.S. Senator, but it is clear that he never intended to do so — Pitkin had broken the inviolable political rule that Mears operated by, that if elected you paid your political debts. After arriving in Denver, Mears became a supporter of another contender, Horace A. W. Tabor, the silver king from Leadville. After ninety-five ballots, Tabor and mining magnate Thomas Bowen remained deadlocked, Pitkin having been left by the wayside. The bitter Tabor-Bowen contest became nationally notorious and was called the "Battle of the Millions" because of the wealth of the two contestants.

The Republican Party believed that if the deadlock continued, it would harm not only Colorado but the country as a whole. Mears was approached by Bowen and was asked (and probably bribed) to change his vote, which he did. He then persuaded other legislators to do the same. Bowen was chosen to fill the longer term, and Tabor the shorter one. A majority of Republicans seem to have approved Mears' action "for the sake of the party." Instead of receiving disapproval, his action was seen as something of a sly and unexpected trick, a joke. The *Rocky Mountain News* named him the "joker in the Republican deck." Tabor supporters, however, vilified Mears in person and in print, and the party discord continued.

It seems that after his one term in the legislature, Mears realized that he could obtain more of what he was after by using influence and money to help control events rather than by seeking election to political office for himself. Running for office and serving if elected Mears saw as a waste of time. A skilled lobbyist willing to use bribery, manipulation, and coercion if necessary could easily influence legislators. Legislators of the time seemed to expect gratuities, and their constituents usually did not object. It was said at the time that Mears became such an effective lobbyist that bills he favored could be counted on to be passed, and those he was against were already defeated just by his disfavor. "His political ideas departed in only one major way from nineteenth century political thought — after 1883, he did not want elective office."[6]

Politics was, for Mears, a means to an end and the end was the power to accomplish what he wanted done, particularly in promoting or protecting his business interests. Inez Hunt's and Wanetta W. Draper's account somewhat exaggeratedly describes the "Little Man with the Giant Stride," "A nod of his head could elect a governor; a flick of his wrist could resettle an entire 'nation'; and his 'X' on the ballot could name the president of the United States."[7]

In May of 1884, Mears was selected by the Republicans of Ouray County to be one of Colorado's representatives at the Republican National Convention in Chicago. It isn't entirely clear whether Mears was a resident of Ouray at the time, but residency had not stood in his way before. When he ran for the state legislature from Saguache County, one of the accusations against him by his opponents was that he was then a resident of Denver. Supporters, however, didn't seem to think that where he resided would affect what Otto Mears could do for them as a legislator.

Also in 1884, Mears determined that a former business associate, William Meyer, would make a tractable — and electable — candidate for governor. The *Rocky Mountain News* reported that Mears "came [to the Republican Convention] with a bundle, and is prepared to pay any reasonable price for Meyer delegates. Otto don't carry anything less than $50. Tap him for one and you may get two if you kick."[8] Mears was not the only big spender in this campaign. The *Rocky Mountain News* asserted that this was the most corrupt Colorado election to date, and that was saying something. However, in spite of efforts by Mears and others, and a great deal of political maneuvering, Benjamin Eaton won the Republican nomination for governor. Mears tried again two years later, in 1886, with his characteristic determination. Mears played his politics better this time and succeeded in getting Meyer nominated to the Republican slate. Even though a Republican nominee was practically assured election in Colorado at this time, the voters apparently did not approve of "a German-born candidate with a Mexican wife backed by a Russian Jew,"[9] and the Democratic slate headed by Alva Adams was voted in by a wide margin. Two years later, the Republicans regained the state offices they had lost in the 1886 campaign, but apparently Mears had given up trying to get Meyer elected.

In the 1888 election, Mears was intent on ensuring defeat for Thomas Bowen. Mears felt that Bowen had betrayed the favor Mears had done for him in Bowen's 1884 bid for United States Senate. Bowen had also been instrumental in the defeat of Meyer, Mears' candidate for governor in 1884. In 1888, Mears was supporting a candidate who promised Mears that he would vote against Bowen. David Frakes Day (even though a Democrat) was Mears' best friend and owner of the Ouray newspaper the *Solid Muldoon,* and Day was strongly in favor of the Democratic candidate. To combat Day in print, Mears started two newspapers, the Ironton *Pacific Slope* and the *Ouray Plaindealer.*[10] Mears' candidate won the election, and Mears was on hand in Denver in January 1889 to help maneuver the defeat of Thomas Bowen for the U.S. Senate seat.

In April 1889, Mears was appointed to the Colorado Board of Capitol Managers, a group assigned to plan and construct a new Colorado State Capitol Building. Determined to overcome earlier mismanagement on the board, Mears took an active role until the capitol building was finished some fifteen years later.

Aside from the Board of Capitol Managers, Mears spent the next few years working primarily on railroad construction, and after the silver crash of 1893, on frantic efforts to recoup his financial losses. Politics, however, were never entirely laid aside. In early 1891, Mears

The Colorado State Capitol Building, soon after completion. Otto Mears was on the Board of Capitol Managers, responsible for its construction, for over thirty years.

was in Denver to work against passage of legislation that would generally restrict railroad construction and operation. This was only the beginning of two decades of Mears' lobbying against railroad legislation. There was strong public support in favor of tightening the laws on railroad financing, but Mears and his investors, along with the major railroad companies, were against any laws limiting their activities.

Colorado had, of course, been established in the wild boom and bust atmosphere of the "rush" beginning in 1859. Even by 1888, when state statistics began to be kept, seventy-eight to ninety-eight-hour work weeks were the norm, although women were generally restricted to only sixty hours. Unheard of were a minimum wage, protection as to number of work hours required, child labor laws, paid vacations, worker's compensation in case of injury or illness, or any mine safety and inspection laws. As late as 1900, the Colorado Supreme Court ruled an attempt by the Colorado General Assembly to regulate hours of work unconstitutional. With reduction of long working hours as a primary motive, between 1888 and 1900, union membership tripled. Otto Mears fought unionization, especially for the railroads, with every weapon in his political arsenal.

The railroads, even though they were the arena for Mears' battles to stop the unions, were the earliest businesses in Colorado in which unionization was successful. The locomotive engineers started forming local unions in 1876, and the firemen did so in 1877. By 1888 the railroad unions were the largest and most effective unions in the state. Nevertheless, company owners including Mears had their heels dug in and they fought tooth and nail to prevent further legal encroachment on their freedom to manipulate legislation and employment on Colorado railroads.

In April 1891, Otto Mears, as President of the Rio Grande Southern Railway; a fellow political activist, Jerry Franz; the Honorable Fred Walsen; ex-Senator A. M. Stevenson; and the Honorable Edwin Mitchell were all indicted by the Arapahoe County Grand Jury for bribery and attempted bribery of members of the Eighth General Assembly. It was a sensational state political scandal. Mears had been lobbying to pack the Legislature's Railroad Committee with legislators favorable to the railroad owners and against restrictive railroad legislation. The specific accusation against Mears was that he had tried to bribe C. B. Bowman, a Representative from Huerfano County, to support a motion to have James W. Hanna made Speaker of the House.

A committee of the legislature investigated, and the majority report as given in the *Denver Times* said:

> *"From the evidence taken by your committee, we are of the opinion that when the members of the House first came together they were assailed by as bold and corrupt a lobby as ever disgraced the history of legislation; that it was provided with an abundance of money, and expected to control thereby the patronage of the State."* [11]

Newspapers, particularly in the southwestern part of the state, stood strongly for Mears and against Bowman, not because they did not believe Mears capable of bribery, but because Bowman's accusation of a bribe of "only" $500 seemed out of character for Mears. The scandal deepened when Mears was accused of tampering with members of the Grand Jury. Countercharges by Mears appeared in the paper saying that the accusations were politically motivated, but neither public opinion nor the views of the Grand Jury were changed.

The *Denver Times* reported:

> *"I know absolutely nothing about it," was [Mears'] invariable answer to every form of an inquiry in regard to his recent indictment. Attempts to enlighten him in regard to the grand jury's action were equally unavailing. Mr. Mears was not to be induced to abandon the bliss of his present condition by anything not official. "These kind of things trouble me very little. I don't bother my head — not the worth of a cigar — over the whole business. It amounts to nothing whatever. But then I know nothing about it. They might publish all sorts of things."* [12]

The primary charge of bribery was finally dropped when Mears' lawyers pointed out an inconsistency. The indictment accused Mears of offering Bowman a $500 bribe on January 9 to vote for Mr. Hanna for speaker, but Hanna had already been elected speaker on January 7. A new Grand Jury was impaneled that dropped that bribery charge, but pressed a second attempted bribery charge. With only one witness against him, Mears was able to convince the second Grand Jury of his innocence.

In the late 1880s and early 1890s, the entire United States was in an economic depression. On top of that, Colorado was so dependent on the silver economy that every fluctuation in the price of silver directly affected the state's economic life. Silver pricing had been varying and contentious since mid-century because of the federal government's attempts to determine the price. Since 1861, the price of silver had been pegged to that of gold, 15.988 ounces of silver per ounce of gold. In 1873, the U.S. Congress legislated a new unit of currency permitting the coinage of gold dollars, but the Bland-Allison Act of 1878, passed over President Hayes' veto, restored limited silver coinage, this time at market price, not pegged to gold. By 1881, Colorado was the leading producer of silver in the United States, and by 1886, the U.S. Senators from Colorado were advocating legislation to allow the unlimited coinage of silver. In 1890, The United States Congress made a move half-way toward removing the silver coinage limitation by passing the Sherman Silver Purchase Act which guaranteed that the government would buy fifty-four million ounces of silver a year. This drove silver prices to over a dollar an ounce. More silver mines were opened up, glutting the market and driving prices back down. A heavy blow fell when the British government announced in June 1893 that they would not mint any more silver coins in India. The price of silver dropped even more and mines began to close. At the same time, national gold reserves dropped, businessmen panicked, and unemployment and bank failures multiplied. It was almost a death knell to the Colorado economy when President Grover Cleveland decided to combat the national depression by repealing the Sherman Silver Purchase Act. In short, in 1888, silver at market price was at $.93 per ounce, rose to over one dollar in 1889, went back down to $.83 in 1893 after the British withdrawal, and plunged to $.63 per ounce after the repeal of the Sherman Act. Without government price support, the silver economy crashed and so did Colorado.

Most of Mears' capital was tied up in railroads at this time, so he was relatively safe. But so much of Colorado's economy, including the railroads, was dependent on silver that he had trouble paying his business debts. In the autumn of 1893 Mears traveled to the East Coast distributing promotional materials in many of the large cities to advocate a national return to the silver standard. He continued to campaign for the silver standard for several years, believing it a solution to Colorado's, and his own, economic woes.

In the election of 1894 Mears again deeply involved himself in state politics, seeking to defeat then Populist Governor Davis H. Waite, running for reelection. Waite had tried to remove Mears from the Board of Capitol Managers, and Mears refused to resign. The issue went as far as the Colorado Supreme Court, which allowed Mears to retain his position on the Board. Mears sponsored a relative unknown, Albert McIntire, for governor, and through heavy campaigning succeeded in winning McIntire the Republican nomination. Serious bribery and coercion were used by the Republicans in trying to get McIntire elected. Combined with public dissatisfaction with Waite and Democratic defection from the previous Democrat-Populist coalition, the Republicans won.

In September of 1896, the Republicans nominated William McKinley for President, but McKinley was in favor of the gold standard, and his Democratic opponent, William Jennings Bryan, supported the silver standard. This so-called "Battle of the Standards" turned the usual political alliances in Colorado upside down. "Silver Republicans," including Mears, broke from the party, formed a separate slate of nominees, and joined the Democrats in support of Bryan. The National Silver Party joined the Populists. Through the Silver Republican Convention and its joint convention with the Democrats immediately following, Mears was a constant voice. One committee member suggested that Mears be chosen as the gubernatorial nominee. Knowing that Mears did not want this, but knowing Mears would enjoy the implied approval, another delegate "pointed out that in effect 'Otto Mears *is* the Governor of Colorado.' [Mears] . . . was so delighted by this open acknowledgement of his importance that he repeated the compliment everywhere."[13]

The importance of Mears was also reported by John L. McNeil, one of Mears' business partners on the Rio Grande Southern Railroad:

> One day governor McIntire got on a street car in Denver. When the conductor came to collect his fare the governor found he had not a cent in his pockets.
> "I can't pay," he said, "I have no money with me."
> "Pay or get off," said the conductor.
> "I am the Governor," the Governor said.
> "Can't help that," replied the conductor, "if you were Otto Mears himself you would have to pay or get off.[14]

Thanks to clever campaigning and Coloradoans' overwhelming support of return of the silver standard, the combined Democrat-Silver Republican slate won the state handily. Unfortunately for the silver supporters, Bryan lost the national election.

By the time of the 1898 election, Mears was greatly involved in East-Coast politics, but didn't want to relinquish control in Colorado, so he did considerable traveling back and forth. For the next five years, until 1903, Mears was primarily involved in banking and other investment interests in Denver, and in completion of the Chesapeake Beach Railway project near Washington, D.C., for David H. Moffat. Mears got involved in his usual way in Maryland state politics and national elections. But after years of struggling financially and fighting litigation, Mears and other company officers were replaced on the Chesapeake Beach Railway. Mears' disillusionment did not last long, and within months he was writing to Fred Walsen, "You can never tell what changes will come to pass in a man's life that will change the entire future."[15] Mears cleared up his affairs on the East Coast, returned briefly to Colorado, and then launched a railroad project between Monroe and New Iberia, Louisiana. During this period of his life he became a "Louisiana Democrat" to obtain the political backing he needed in that state for his business interests. A competitor outmaneuvered Mears on the railroad, and the venture was not a success. During this time, Mears spent nine months as president of the Mack Brothers Motor Car Company and became fascinated by the idea of a "rail car," an automobile or truck chassis that would run on his narrow gauge rails.

Mears returned to Colorado in 1906, having been gone a decade, though he visited Colorado frequently. He had lost heavily in both the Chesapeake Beach Railway and his Louisiana railroad project. It was not until 1911 that the little Russian entrepreneur amassed another fortune, this time in mining. Mears had returned in the interim to continue to participate in Colorado politics, being very influential in the election of United States Senator Edward O. Wolcott. Wolcott, however, incurred Mears' enmity through what Mears regarded as Wolcott's ingratitude and double dealing, which culminated when Wolcott successfully outmaneuvered Mears in a Rio Grande Southern stock manipulation.[16] Mears turned his support to Wolcott's opponent, former Senator and Secretary of the Interior Henry Teller.

The battle between Wolcott and Teller was so furious that it almost split the Republican Party in Colorado. It was a wild time, which included election fraud, party splitting, double dealing, armed thugs hired to intimidate legislators, attempts by Democrats and Republicans to unseat each other in the House and Senate, and essentially a "sit-in" in the Senate chambers by Senators who feared that if they left, they would never be allowed back in. On January 20, Governor James H. Peabody debated calling out the state militia to control a disorderly throng surrounding the capitol building, and National Guard units assembled at the Armory. When things finally settled down to a vote, it was deadlocked between Wolcott and Teller. More politicking and attempts at trickery occurred including the Democrats trying to trick the Republicans into leaving, perhaps by declaring a recess, so that the Democrats could call an emergency session without the Republicans and elect their man. Many legislators went armed until a joint session could be opened on January 23.

In a blatantly illegal series of maneuvers, the Democrats finally pushed through Teller. Wolcott was so angry he sought revenge against those Republicans who had failed to back him. He began by seeking to have Mears and others thrown out of the Republican Party. The Arapahoe County Central Committee voted by a large majority to suspend Mears and three others from the Republican Party for two years. They believed that this vote and subsequent publicity, which they would ensure, would guarantee that the Colorado Republican Party would oust Mears and the other three affected members. Mears and the others forestalled the action with a successful appeal to the Republican Union Club. Mears immediately began to restore good relations by hosting a series of banquets with Republican Party members as guests. One such banquet, for example, was a ten-dollar-a-plate dinner in the ballroom of the Adams Hotel in Denver which thirty-five of the forty Republican members of the House attended.

Good relations restored, Mears continued to lobby against business reform legislation. Legislators had begun to introduce many bills designed to correct the abuses of big business and government. Mears fought strongly, for example, against a bill that would have stipulated that eight per cent of voters who had voted in a previous gubernatorial election could initiate legislation and that citizens could vote on the acceptability of measures already approved by the legislature. Mears realized that such legislation would virtually end the ability of politicians and big businessmen to control of the affairs of the state by giving some of their power to the voting public. In another effort, Mears helped prevent passage of a constitutional amendment allowing the University of Denver to establish a medical school in Denver. One might ask why Mears would object to such a measure. In fact, it was not the measure itself but the mere fact of changing the constitution that Mears objected to. Political bosses in Colorado wanted to maintain a weak legislature that they could manipulate, so they certainly did not want the elected officials to discover that with the voters' approval they had the power even to amend the state's constitution. Next, Mears helped defeat a tax reform measure. If it had passed, the poor would have paid less tax, and the burden would be shifted to big business. Mears similarly worked to defeat a bill calling for an eight-hour work day and one calling for regulation of the smelting industry.

It is obvious that Mears and his associates were driven by self-centered economic concerns and the desire to maintain their own political power. There appears to have been little consideration for the working man or the general citizenry. Mears and his associates were out to control Colorado politics and to make money, and they fought hard, using any means foul or fair (but prudent enough to avoid incarceration) to defeat legislation that would have hindered them in their efforts.

Back in 1899 Mears had lobbied in a new arena — as a Capitol Manager, he was involved in the selection of deceased pioneers to be honored in the dome of the state capitol. He wasn't deceased, but he believed that he had done as much as any other pioneer, so he sought to have a memorial to himself established somewhere in the capitol. He not only put forth a publicity campaign for himself, but he presented or had presented a petition to provide a gallery for living pioneers — the first one to be Otto Mears. It took years, and much wrestling with opponents, but finally in 1904, a stained-glass portrait of Otto Mears was placed on the outside corridor of the second and third floors of the Colorado State Capitol building. The authorization for the window, written in 1901, stated:

> *Whereas, Hon. Otto Mears, during the entire time of the construction of this State Capitol of Colorado has been a member of the Board of Capitol Managers, and through his energy, zeal and executive ability had largely contributed to the erection of the noble edifice which is a source of pride to all citizens of the state, and . . . . Whereas, Mr. Mears during residence of nearly 40 years in the state,*

with generous devotion to its interests, has been connected with and initiated many public enterprises tending to pro- mote its welfare, develop its resources and to its material wealth, and has, it being a well recognized fact, done more than any other single individual, by the construction of roads, railroads and otherwise to open for settlement and development an immense area in Southwestern Colorado, comprising a large portion of the state, whereby happy homes have been furnished to many thousands of prosper- ous citizens and that taxable wealth of the state increased by millions; . . . Now, therefor [sic], be it Resolved, by the Senate and House of the thirteenth General Assembly of Colorado, that Hon. Otto Mears is in the opinion of this General Assembly worthy to be thus honored; and the Board of Capitol Managers is hereby requested to cause his portrait to be placed in the Capitol dome or some suitable place in the Capitol Building . . . .[17]

Mears never admitted all the political effort he'd had to go through to receive this singular honor.

Mears declared himself done with politics in 1905. He said to a reporter from the *Denver Republican,* "I am out of politics. I have had my share. My skin is about as thick as you make 'em, but I find that it feels better to be out of it and making money. Do you know that I am getting old?"[18]

Within a few months, however, Mears had been recruited by his old friend and protégé Simon Guggenheim, "the smelter king," to assist him in the next senatorial election. Guggenheim was hungering for Thomas Patterson's seat, which would be vacated in 1907. Guggenheim was willing, apparently, to spend any amount of money to win it. In order to help Guggenheim, Mears needed to reinstate his Colorado res- idency, which he did by purchasing a home on Reese Street in Silverton, allegedly his ninth legal residence at the time.[19]

On January 1, 1907, a Republican caucus at the Brown Palace Hotel in Denver confirmed Guggenheim's nomination, with sixty-eight of seventy votes. Since the Republicans held the legislature it was assumed that Guggenheim was a sure winner. The newspapers of the state implied it, and the more liberal newspapers decried the use of influence and money to win the seat, even before it was won. The edi-

A natty-looking Republican power broker, Otto Mears, in a drawing from a familiar photograph.

tor of the *Colorado Springs Gazette*, the oldest Republican newspaper in Colorado, wrote, "Simon Guggenheim in the United States Senate would be a joke, but a most discreditable joke on Colorado. He would be simply a dollar mark placed there to show that another state had sold out."[20]

Mears and Guggenheim, meanwhile, continued on their planned course, particularly watching the Colorado legislature to try to avert passage of any bills that would further regulate big business, especially the railroads. Republicans had promised in the campaign to frame a strong railroad commission law that would force the railroads to reduce rates and give better service. Ticket prices on the railroads were so high that working people could not afford to ride them. On the eve of the day when the proposed measure to create a railroad commission was to have been considered, railroad passes were left on the desk of each legislator. It was rumored that assemblymen could also expect further favors from the railroads. Usually railroad passes were accepted without comment by the legislators as, even with a fifteen-cent mileage allowance for a round-trip ticket to Denver during the legislative session, remuneration for legislators barely covered their expenses.

Occasionally an honest legislator (they appear to have been few and far between) would object to a free railroad pass, and in this case Representative Kem from Montrose objected. He said that no other state was as dominated by big business as was Colorado. Kem reported this incident to the newspapers and wrote a letter to the president of each railroad whose pass had appeared on legislators' desks. He returned his passes. Public sentiment was aroused and a bill creating a railroad commission was finally voted into law. To save his own business, Mears immediately got a judge to declare narrow gauge short lines like his — his three lines out of Silverton together totaled less than fifty miles — exempt from the new regulation.

The reports of lobbying against railroad legislation caused some loss of public favor toward Guggenheim. He furthered his own descent in popularity by arrogant remarks about political bargains that would ensure his election. His popular support dropped so much that some of his supporters in the legislature were hesitant to vote for him, fearing loss of their own elected offices. Mears pointed out to the Republicans that it had been Guggenheim's money that had paid the party's campaign costs in the last several elections. In the end, Guggenheim was elected, but Otto Mears' participation in politics dwindled after the election. Guggenheim himself, in a May 18, 1907, announcement, expressed his ambitions to control state politics by usurping the power of his old mentor. Mears, however, is known to have done some manipulation of Guggenheim of his own while Guggenheim was in office. Otto Mears hadn't lost his touch.

Mary Mears was by now in poor health, and much of Otto's time was spent with her in California. However, he was still on the Board of Capitol Managers, which had become politically an important government agency. Even after the capitol building was completed, the board continued to act, discussing improvements to the capitol and even at one time plans for a new museum. It always acted as a distributor of political patronage and jobs for supporters of the dominant political party. The Board at one time even awarded contracts to those who offered the largest bribes, rather than the lowest bids. In 1914, Governor George A. Carlson called for a Grand Jury investigation of several government agencies. Their report caused the legislature to attempt to abolish the Board for reasons of corruption and incompetence, not to mention the point that since the Capitol had been completed years before, it had no real purpose.

The Board narrowly survived the legislature, but funding was reduced and the Board lost much of its ability to offer patronage, and hence lost much of its power. Mears was not directly implicated in any malfeasance, and he remained on the board until 1920.

Even in Mears' time, bribery, coercion, manipulation, and dishonesty were not in any way considered moral. Mears was undoubtedly good at such activity, and he made money and gained power with it, but unless one believes money and power to be the highest values, Mears' political life cannot be given the attribute of morality. In politics, Mears' actions to support his own business interests and to make money were often obviously corrupt and hard to justify.

CHAPTER 6

Audacious Little Narrow-Gauge Lines

O tto Mears and his three short-line railroads cannot be better presented than by the Introduction to the lavishly illustrated book by Sloan and Skowronski, *The Rainbow Route:*

> [The Rainbow Route] *is the story of three small narrow-gauge railroads with an aggregate length of less than 50 miles, which operated for all too brief a period of time in the harsh, but magnificent mountain canons and high sub-alpine country of southwestern Colorado. Their construction involved steeper grades and tighter curves than any other mountain railroad in North America, save one — the Uintah. And they met a need that not even the aggressive and powerful Denver and Rio Grande (D&RG) was ever bold enough to fill.*
>
> *This audacious trio of little narrow-gauge lines came about principally through the efforts of one highly practical dreamer, Otto Mears, in association with his poker-playing cronies — and survived as very much a family business. These lines were solely responsible for the profitability of some 20 mines during the 55 years they were in existence; and as such, they were directly or indirectly responsible for the livelihood of about 200,000 people, including most of the inhabitants of San Juan County, as well as a goodly number in Ouray County — and a few daring outside investors . . . .*
>
> *They had few major accidents and only one fatality; their histories reveal that most of their lives consisted of conflicts with the blind perversity of economics, the elements, and the D&RG. They began running where primitive wagon roads had led — and only when motor trucks at last were strong and sturdy enough to replace*

them, were they finally considered no longer useful, and subjected to the indignity of being ripped apart and abandoned forevermore. [1]

The mighty Denver and Rio Grande Railroad (D&RG RR) was given birth in 1870 under the leadership of General William J. Palmer. When Colorado, because of its terrain as well as some failed politicking, lost out to Wyoming on its bid for the transcontinental railroad route, Palmer built the Denver Pacific as a branch line from the transcontinental rails in Wyoming to the territorial capital at Denver. The Denver and Rio Grande was intended to continue to reach south from Denver for access to the Mexican railroads. The D&RG was narrow gauge from the beginning, and the three-foot track (instead of the standard gauge four-feet, eight-and-one-half inches), with its little locomotives, proved the answer to Colorado's mountainous regions. By 1880, eastern Colorado was well served by the D&RG and other growing railroads.

Also by 1880, legal territorial conflicts between the Denver and Rio Grande and the Atchison, Topeka and Santa Fe Railroads had been settled, and the D&RG was free to start building a line to Leadville to take advantage of the enormous silver boom there. Soon Leadville-bound passengers could make their way to the new mines on the Denver and South Park rails over Fremont Pass or on the D&RG through the Royal Gorge. The D&RG won a race with the South Park by driving its lines to Gunnison in the late summer of 1881, and the line was extended to Grand Junction by way of Montrose in 1883. Soon, the D&RG built a line running south from Montrose to Dallas (near present-day Ridgway) and then to Ouray. On the southern side of the San Juans, D&RG track ran west across the southern part of southwestern Colorado from Alamosa, arriving in Durango in 1881, and on up from Durango to Silverton the next year. But the D&RG said that to extend the line north from Silverton into the mining areas was unfeasible. Nevertheless, as Duane Smith points out, the San Juans "did not remain the Denver and Rio Grande's private fiefdom; the challenge came from none other than Otto Mears." [2]

It may appear as though Otto Mears was kept busy full time with his road building, mercantile businesses, mail delivery, politics, and work with the Ute Indians, yet even these activities did not completely fill his time. In the late 1870s in Saguache, Mears became involved in an activity that would have a major effect on his life — railroads. He acted as the agent for the D&RG at Saguache and that employment served as his introduction to the arena that would change his life, and that of the San Juans.

By the mid 1880s, all the towns in the San Juans were growing. Silverton had as many as 1,500 people, but Ouray was the largest town in the region, having such relatively easy access from the north. In the mid 1880s, Ouray boasted a population of 1,800, with two hotels, two newspapers (the *Ouray Times* and the *Solid Muldoon*), mining operations, three churches, and a school. Into this exciting setting in the heart of the San Juan Mountains came Otto Mears to create and finance his "Rainbow Route," beginning with his marvelous little narrow gauge "short-line," the Silverton Railroad.

We hear little of Mears having any interest in railroads for the decade after 1875, except when he was building wagon roads to intersect nearby branches of the D&RG north and west of Saguache. In the meantime, Mears got heavily involved in the packing and freighting business. In the early 1880s he decided it would be profitable to freight ore down from Red Mountain into Silverton, which the D&RG had reached in the summer of 1882. In October 1884, Mears, Fred Walsen, and Silverton investor J. L. Pennington incorporated the Mears Transportation Company. In the very beginning the firm was capitalized with only $6000, but with increased capital, it soon was said to be the largest freighting company in Colorado. In 1885 the company hauled 12,550 tons of ore from Red Mountain. In 1886 the capital stock was raised to $50,000 so that more teams and wagons could be bought. With this equipment, the company shipped 18,150 tons of Red Mountain ore in 1886 and even more in 1887. [3]

Moving around the country was no easy task in those days. People traveled mostly by foot or by horseback, and stagecoaches were frequently used where there were roads. Winter travel was always a problem. Some used long skis, which they called snowshoes, with a single, long pole for steering. A few miners had been known to sled (today we might call it snowboarding!) down the slopes from the mine on a shovel to be in town in time for Saturday night festivities. Getting back up to the mine the next day was considerably more difficult. Avalanches were a constant danger to man and beast. In the spring of 1891, for example, the infamous Riverside Slide south of Ouray ran several times, eventually covering 480 feet of road. A tunnel was dug through the slide, and as more snow and ice slid over the surface it rose to 100 feet above the tunnel. The tunnel was large enough for stagecoaches, and was still in use in July of that year.

Moving freight — supplies and equipment up to the mines, and ore back down — was even more difficult. Ken Reyher reports in *Silver and Sawdust:*

> *Most of the ore bodies were at or above timberline, more than two miles above sea level. Heavy mining machinery had to be moved up to the mines and the ore had to be hauled back down. Working personnel usually lived at the site so building materials, food, and coal also had to be transported up the mountain. Supply centers were established in the valleys, and for the first few years, until railroads were built, everything needed had to be freighted in by wagon and then packed in on the backs of burros or mules for the final miles up to the diggings.* [4]

Railroads were clearly the answer. Even though they were expensive to construct, they could haul far greater loads, they were much more efficient, and freighting rates by rail were often between one-half and one-third the cost by wagon or one-tenth the cost by pack load. Knowing all this, however, everyone did not always appreciate the railroads. For example, concerning the Rio Grande Southern, which ran from Ridgway to Durango, Reyher reports:

> *One story that was repeated for years in the Telluride area related to a verbal exchange between a very pregnant passenger and the conductor. The agitated woman demanded the train go faster as she was going into labor. The exasperated conductor told the lady that she should have had better sense than to have even gotten on the train in that condition. Her terse reply was that she had not been pregnant prior to boarding.* [5]

"As every narrow-gauge rail fan will tell you, the Mears lines in the San Juans were the quintessence of this quaintest of railroad forms — charming, irresponsible, unpredictable," [6] said Marshall Sprague. Mears' first line, the Silverton Railroad, which ran from the town of that name to Red Mountain, cost twice as much per mile to build as the less mountainous lines in Colorado. An additional financial disadvantage incurred was that the high mountain railroads often could not run in winter. Yet rail transport was still far cheaper for the shippers and able to provide a handsome profit.

Before getting into railroading, Mears used some of the income from the Mears Transportation Company and his toll roads to invest in various mining and town planning schemes. One abortive scheme involved the Ramona Town Company, incorporated in December 1886. The company's purpose was to lay out a town site and sell lots to settlers. Ramona was to be located only four miles north of Ouray, but because of the terrain, Ramona was much more easily accessed from Montrose than Ouray. Dave Day and Otto Mears figured that when the D&RG came south out of Montrose, Ramona would be an ideal terminus, the last four miles into Ouray being so difficult for construction of a rail line. However, the president of the D&RG, David Moffat, after being invited to Ouray to be wined and dined, offered the citizens of Ouray the extension of the railroad to their town if they would raise the necessary funds, and the people of Ouray eagerly concurred. Ramona was doomed. Settlers saw no reason to move to an undeveloped spot when Ouray was just four miles away. The directors of the Ramona Town Company dissolved the company and returned the money to those who had purchased lots, but they lost money on the deal. Ramona became the site of David Day's farm and ranch. It wasn't until 1907 that the remaining Ramona town-site land was finally sold to J. P. Donovan.

As the 1880s progressed, it became more and more apparent that although Otto Mears had a financial finger in the shipping and freighting pie throughout the San Juans, he could profit by moving into railroads. The need for cheap transportation was increasing, especially in the movement of great quantities of ore from the mines. The only feasible way to move such quantities was by rail.

Early in 1887, then, Mears looked closely into the situation at Red Mountain and Silverton to see about building a railroad to bring the huge tonnage of Red Mountain ore down to the D&RG terminus at Silverton. With the efficiencies of rail transport, lower grade ore could also be profitably shipped to the smelters. So in the late 1800s, Mears built the Silverton Railroad from Silverton north and west to Red Mountain Town, Ironton, and Albany; the Rio Grande Southern from Ridgway by Telluride, Rico, and Dolores around to Durango, and the Silverton Northern from Silverton north and east to Animas Forks. In the late 1890s, he even built two railroads far to the east, the Chesapeake Beach Railway near Washington D.C. and a line between Monroe and New Iberia, Louisiana.

Even though the D&RG had earlier declared a rail line north from Silverton either to Red Mountain and Ironton or to Eureka to be unprofitable (and perhaps even unbuildable), Mears and other officers of the new company were convinced that such a railroad could pay, and handsomely. Despite a good deal of skepticism in the communities, the company incorporated the Silverton Railroad Company in July and within two weeks, track laying had started on the narrow-gauge track following Mears' toll-road bed. Because of bad weather, they were able to lay only a little over five miles that season, from Silverton to so-called Burro Bridge on the walking trail to Ophir. Even Dave Day, Mears' close friend, expressed doubt about the feasibility of the route: "Mears will wake up some storming morning and find that his Silverton-Chattanooga summer route has bumped up against one of the Polar region's semi-daily slides and gone over to Ophir on a vacation."[7]

In November 1887, the Silverton Railroad bought its first locomotive from the Denver and Rio Grande, an overhauled Baldwin, for $6,500. Mears gave it the number 100 and the name *Ouray*. The Silverton later rented additional engines from the D&RG and the soon-to-be-built Rio Grande Southern Railroad.

In early 1888, Mears was preparing his famous railroad passes for use on the line. All railroads issued paper passes, but Mears wanted to do something more extravagant. He began with two-and-one-half by four-inch buckskin passes, and in 1889 issued silver passes stamped with a mountain railroad scene. In 1890, he issued oval watch fobs or medallions also made of silver. Three years later, he issued passes made of silver or gold filigree for the exclusive use of patrons on his Rio Grande Southern and Silverton railroads. The passes became collectors' items but unfortunately today only a hundred or so are known to still exist. The Saguache County Museum has a beautifully preserved silver and gold pass issued on The Silverton Railroad Company for 1809 to I. Gotthelf. The pass is imprinted with "No. 46" and the embossed signature of Otto Mears.

The only gold watch-fob railroad pass made by Mears was given to Rasmus Hanson, a Danish immigrant who had come through Quebec and Chicago to strike it rich in the San Juans. After he made his fortune, Hanson married a Denver girl and built a home in Silverton. The railroad

Table 1: Otto Mears' San Juan Railroads

Railroad	Route	Begun	Completed	Length (mi.)	Years in Service	Notes
Silverton	Silverton to Red Mountain and on to Ironton and Albany via Mineral Creek, Chattanooga, and Corkscrew Gulch turntable	July 1887	Sept. 1888, Summer 1889*	22.5	33 (parts of the line)	Spurs to Yankee Girl, Guston, Vanderbilt, North Star, Silver Bell, and National Belle Mines and Treasury Tunnel
Rio Grande Southern	Dallas (Ridgway) to Telluride, Rico, Dolores, and Durango	Oct. 1890	Nov. 1891	162	Sold to D&RG, 1895	Served mining and ranching camps of Placerville, Ophir, Telluride, Rico
Silverton Northern	Silverton up Animas River to Howardsville and Eureka	1895**, 1904***	1896**, 1904***	13.8	44	Howardsville, Eureka, Animas Forks
Silverton, Gladstone & Northerly	Silverton up Cement Creek to Gladstone	Apr, 1899	July, 1899****	8	Approx. 20	Gold King Mill

* to Albany
** to Eureka
*** to Animas Forks and the Old Hundred Mine
**** Built by others. Mears leased the line in 1910, bought it in 1915.

pass is imprinted with the statement that its gold is from the Sunnyside Extension Mine (owned by Hanson) and that it is for use on the Silverton Railroad. To top it all off, it had a ruby inset into its surface.

One of Mears' triumphs was hiring Charles Wingate Gibbs as his chief engineer. Gibbs had worked in railroad construction on the Colorado Front Range, most recently around Colorado Springs. The combination of Mears' entrepreneurial vision and willingness to test new technological ideas, and Gibbs' engineering brilliance and innovation, was invaluable in the creation of railroads believed by most to be impossible.

After graduation from Maine State College with a degree in civil engineering in 1879, Gibbs had gone to work as an assistant to Thomas Wigglesworth on the Colorado Midland Railroad. Gibbs had enough engineering savvy to know when the hallowed practices of railroad design could be ignored, and with Mears' concurrence, he created tracks where others could not conceive it possible. The road from Burro Bridge on up to Red Mountain included the Muleshoe Curve just beyond Chattanooga where the railroad rose 550 feet in a quarter of a mile as the crow flies, climbing up Mill Creek and then making a 200 degree curve with a 194-foot radius, and all in a five percent grade (that is, a rise or decline of five feet for every hundred feet of track). Travelers today traverse much this same corner on U.S. Highway 550, also known as the "Million Dollar Highway."

Proceeding north, the Silverton required three major bridges and four more near-180-degree curves. Some of the curves went from the level to a five percent grade in sixty feet. The Silverton Railroad topped the pass and reached Red Mountain Town in September 1888. Many of the small settlements scattered around Red Mountain Town almost immediately began to lose population as residents moved to the railroad center at Red Mountain Town, or other towns like Guston and Ironton that would also be on the tracks. In Red Mountain Town, because there was really only one flat area, the depot was uniquely built within the wye. An outhouse was also placed within the wye so that travelers in urgent need would not have to wait on cars being switched to get to the toilet facilities quickly.

On the continuation on the Silverton Railroad down to Ironton, Charles Gibbs made history with the switchback at Corkscrew Gulch. Since there was not room for a standard curve, a turntable (later covered because of the snow) was located by Gibbs and Mears on the main track to make the extremely tight corner. Carla Black wrote, "Only a soaring pioneering spirit would conceive such a creative solution to what would have been fatal flaws in building a railroad for anyone but Otto Mears."[8]

The Corkscrew Gulch turntable was built on a switchback where the grades were four percent. It was designed specifically to fit engine 100, the *Ouray*. When backing, the *Ouray* had poor traction, especially in snow, and it was already reaching its load limit when hauling two loaded ore cars back up the steep grade from Ironton. To negotiate the switchback, the *Ouray* needed to be reversed, but there was no room for a loop, a wye, or even a siding. In less than two months' construction, Gibbs created a working turntable using a unique gravity feed.[9] The two tracks from Red Mountain and from Ironton both sloped slightly down hill to the turntable. The tracks were nearly parallel by the time they reached the switch onto the single line entering the turntable. Unhooked from the cars before the two tracks converged, the locomotive steamed onto the turntable and was turned around, and then it was driven onto the other line. The cars were gently allowed by gravity to coast onto the single line, and even onto the turntable a bit, with careful attention to the brakes so they wouldn't keep on going and career across the turntable and into the gulch several hundred feet below. Then the *Ouray* was backed up, hooked onto the cars (which were now traveling backwards from the way they started out), and the little train proceeded on down, or up, the line. The whole process took only five minutes to perform.

When asked why Mears didn't buy a new bi-directional locomotive, he bragged that the turntable was more cost-effective than a new engine would have been. In fact, the turntable cost $6,000 and the new locomotive would have been only $6,500. One might guess that both Mears and Gibbs were greatly taken with the idea of designing and building this creative turntable. It's also apparent that Mears was fond of the *Ouray* engine itself — he often had himself photographed with it.

It is still possible to hike to the Corkscrew turntable site, although it is not obvious how to get there. The site is also visible from across the gulch on the Corkscrew four-wheel-drive road. Time and vandals have left only enough of the turntable for railroad buffs to see the main wheels of the table and smaller wheels on which it turned.

The Silverton Railroad reached Ironton in November 1888. The extension from Ironton to Albany, one and one-half miles, was completed in the summer of 1889. Total construction and equipment costs

The unique Corkscrew Gulch turntable in the line between Red Mountain Town and Ironton — as it originally appeared and as it remains today.

amounted to $725,000, an almost unbelievable amount for the time. Auxiliary tracks were built out to the surrounding mines — the Vanderbilt, Yankee Girl, Guston, Silver Bell, and the Joker.

Mears dreamed and planned for years to extend the Silverton Railroad from Ironton to Ouray, and he even drew up elaborate plans for an electric railroad in the late nineteenth century and continued to work on them as late as 1905, but to no avail. That project was beyond the capability of Otto Mears and his innovative engineer, Charles Gibbs. Even if it had become technically possible, the silver crash in 1893 closed so many mines that after that time, such a project would no longer have been economically worthwhile. Except for the eight miles from Ironton to Ouray, Mears' Rainbow Route, combined with the Denver and Rio Grande's Durango-to-Silverton and Ridgway-to-Ouray lines, would have completed the 243-mile circle now known as the San Juan Scenic Highway.

Soon after completion of the track to Ironton, Charles Gibbs' bride wrote a letter home describing one of the early trips on the Silverton Railroad:

> *Late in September of 1889, Mr. Gibbs and I were married at Colorado Springs and started for Silverton, going by way of Montrose and through Ouray where we stayed overnight at the beautiful Beaumont Hotel. The next morning we rode the stage to Ironton and there transferred to the little Silverton Railroad train. As we climbed the grade toward the summit the conductor came through the coach where I was the only passenger and asked me if I were cold. I couldn't deny it so he stopped the train, picked up some wood along the track, and built a fire in the little pot-bellied stove.*[10]

Mears himself was consumed by the management of the railroad. Dave Day wrote:

> *The Midland Railroad folks should imitate the economic example and precedent followed and established by Otto Mears. Otto is president, general manager, the traffic manager, general passenger agent, auditor, station agent and section boss on the Silverton and Red Mountain railroad.*[11]

Mears seemed fascinated with his railroad and its equipment. He even studied the characteristics of his locomotives and mail, freight, and passenger cars and then named them appropriately. He named one private car "Hill," because it had trouble staying on track. The reference was to Nathaniel Hill, a Republican political boss known for jumping from one side to another in a political battle as it suited him. Mears even bought a luxurious sleeping car for the little two-hour run, the last thing the railroad needed, but it apparently tickled his fancy.

The Rainbow Route describes Mears during this part of his life:

> *Although he consistently wore a business suit, tie and hat, he remained a jack-of-all-trades, and expected his employees to perform in the same manner. The many minor infractions of his employees he would forgive, but abuse of his locomotives was not to be tolerated; engineers were expected to keep their engines in good repair and running condition. Mears often wandered down to the enginehouse, where he just could not keep his hands off the work in progress. When the job was done, he would wash up in the cold water at the enginehouse sink, then pull on his coat, and his tie and hat before he stepped outside to return to other tasks."* [12]

The Silverton Railroad ended up with about twenty-five miles of track including branches to the mines. It shipped coal and supplies that had come to Silverton from Durango up to the mines and towns around Red Mountain, and the emptied cars were then filled with ore to ship back down to smelters in Silverton, Durango, or Denver. The Silverton, as the "originating carrier" on outgoing shipments could net more than two dollars a mile on freight charges. Mears managed to increase his earnings by exaggerating the length of the Silverton Railroad, thereby making a greater profit.

Even after the 1893 silver crash, the continued output from the Guston, Yankee Girl, and other Red Mountain mines, and the shipment of that output to the Silverton smelter, enabled the Silverton Railroad to remain viable for some years and saved Otto Mears from possible bankruptcy.

Mears had Gibbs working on plans for tracks from Ironton toward Ouray in 1889, but by mid-July 1889, Mears turned Gibbs' attention to surveying and grading what would years later become another Mears railroad, the Silverton Northern from Silverton up the Animas River to Eureka.

While Gibbs was starting to plan the Silverton Northern, in the autumn of 1889 Mears turned his attention to what would become perhaps his greatest railroad building feat, the magnificent Rio Grande Southern (RGS). The line from Ouray to Ironton proving impossible (though he never quite gave up on it), Mears turned to a long-held dream of laying track, as much as possible on his old toll roads, to connect the Ouray and the Durango branches of the D&RG. The route would involve a semi-circle from near Ridgway, west over the Dallas Divide to Placerville, up the San Miguel River to connect to a seven-mile branch to Telluride, over the pass to Rico, southwesterly down the Dolores River, and then back around to come into Durango from the west. Charles Gibbs had already surveyed the proposed route between Dallas and Telluride. As the rest of the 162-mile route proved feasible, according to Gibbs' surveys, in early March 1890 the Rio Grande Southern Construction Company was incorporated.

Mears went to the East Coast to raise funds for the Rio Grande Southern, his longest railroad. He was hugely successful at this fund raising, as his reputation for building the already highly profitable Silverton Railroad had preceded him.

Mears returned to Colorado in early 1890 with the money needed to begin. While he had been away, however, land values in Dallas, the little town proposed to be the northern intersection point of the new railroad with the D&RG, had soared. Mears and Fred Walsen moved the junction two and a half miles south and incorporated a new town, originally called Magentie but later Ridgway, after Arthur. M. Ridgway, then construction supervisor of the Denver and Rio Grande Railroad. Later, Ridgway became superintendent of the Rio Grande Southern. The town of Ridgway not only became a railroad center, but a supply center, and a center for agriculture, ranching, and coal, which was available nearby. The town of Dallas declined, and Ridgway boomed.

On his way home from the East Coast in 1890, Mears stopped in Lima, Ohio, at the Lima Machine Works to order a 37-ton, two-truck Shay geared locomotive, shop number "269." This small engine was delivered to the RGS in Durango in mid-April 1890 and was given the same number for the RGS. It was immediately put to work hauling construction supplies on the southern end of the RGS. As soon as the line

Otto Mears poses with his beloved Silverton Railroad Locomotive No. 100, which he named *Ouray*.

reached the Porter Coal Mine five and a half miles out of Durango, No. 269 was used to haul coal during the winter months of 1890-1891, while construction work had to halt because of the snow.[13]

For the most part, Mears personally searched out and eventually purchased or leased most of the engines for the Rio Grande Southern from the D&RG and the Denver and Rio Grande Western, as those lines were beginning to phase out narrow gauge in favor of standard gauge. This meant that the larger railroads were eager to sell or lease out the equipment, but it also meant that the RGS was starting out with older hand-me-down freight locomotives that were frequently in poor working order.

Three problems plagued construction of the Rio Grande Southern — terrain, weather, and workers. The problems with the terrain could be conquered through the engineering genius of Gibbs on the northern end and Thomas Wigglesworth on the southern, and even perhaps to some extent by Mears himself. The northern end climbed gently west out of Ridgway over the Dallas Divide at no more than a four percent grade. The western side of Dallas Divide, however, was more precipitous. As *The R.G.S. Story* puts it, "This part of the railroad proved to be a locomotive engineer's nightmare, resulting in magnificent wrecks, and great skill was required of the crews to handle heavy tonnage downgrade — not to mention the involvement of additional engines used as helpers to haul the tonnage upgrade."[14]

Weather delays from an unusually wet summer could be handled by raising additional funds to cover the expenses. The labor problem, however, was more difficult. Mears had recruited laborers from outside and brought them in, to find that almost immediately, most of the men left the railroad for higher-paying work in the mines. He brought in hundreds of Mexican workers who did excellent work in the summer, but they were not equipped nor accustomed to the high mountain winters and most returned home as winter closed in. Mears began to search as far away as Kansas and Missouri for labor. Although sufficient labor was found, keeping enough men was always a problem. Even though at times he had a thousand men laying track from Durango west, and two thousand men spread between Ridgway and Telluride, there were never enough workmen for the eager Mears. Dave Day wrote: "Otto Mears returned Tuesday from a ride over the Rio Grande Southern . . . . Otto now works 22 hours per day, leaving two hours for sleep and scheming; he never eats."[15]

Mears' hard work paid off and the Rio Grande Southern was completed to Telluride in late November of 1890. Telluride was jubilant, as was Mears. But the completion to Telluride caused another labor problem — the saloons of Telluride were too great a temptation for the laborers working the track south from there, and their extensive imbibing caused slowdowns in the progress of track laying. Besides the "booze" problem, delays were continuously caused by shortages of rails, uncompleted bridges, and crossties that were so green they wouldn't even hold a spike.

During 1890-1891, Mears raised more capital in the East, but was faced with difficulties in terrain that were his greatest challenge to date, with the sole exception of his wagon road through the Uncompahgre Gorge between Ouray and Ironton. About ten miles southwest of Telluride, the only possible route rose precipitously from the San Miguel River valley to the divide between the Dolores and San Miguel drainages. Months were spent trying to find or design a passable route. This led to the construction of the famed Ophir Loop. This engineering marvel had two parts. Two high trestles and one smaller one were built on the lower part. On the upper segment, called the "High Line," four large trestles were built. So difficult was the terrain that the bridges had to be bolted together on the ground and then hauled up over rocks into position using block-and-tackle. When possible, locomotives provided power for hauling the trestle assemblies. The Loop carried the track far back into the Ophir canyon until it reached a place wide enough to make the turn, whence the outward track paralleled the inward, always gaining altitude until it could continue the climb up the pass. When the train finally reached Rico, on the other side of the pass, on September 30, 1891, rejoicing, banquets, and other celebrations marked the event.

Delayed, and concerned that he would be unable to raise more money because of the worsening economic conditions in the nation, Mears worked eighteen hours a day — it is not said how hard he drove his workers — to meet the track being built from Durango. Weather permitted, and the two tracks joined in December 1891. Mears donated fifty turkeys and three barrels of beer for the celebration. Completion of the railroad was directly responsible for greater mining investment and development in the region and for development of the lower elevations for agriculture. Durango gained economically especially in those areas of development as well as in the new coal mining needed to supply the local railroads.

OTTO MEARS' RAILROADS

NORTH

0   10   20   30

MILES

(RGS) RIO GRANDE SOUTHERN   (SN) SILVERTON NORTHERN

(SGN) SILVERTON, GLADSTONE & NORTHERLY   (S) SILVERTON

At first, the RGS was profitable, not only because of hauling supplies to the many mines and mining communities on the route, but also by making use of resources along the route — particularly timber and the coal from the Porter Mine near Durango that supplied the needs of the RGS, Mears' short lines out of Silverton, and the local needs of the D&RG.

During 1891, Mears decided that Durango would make the best location for the headquarters of his railroad center. He had notions of extending the Rio Grande Southern westward, heading for Phoenix and even Los Angeles. The Arizona fruit industry was particularly interested, as they were limited by spoilage in trying to ship fruit to distant markets by slower means. Because of his move, Mears wanted Durango to grow, and he engaged in buying and selling real estate and advertising the town. He even worked to convince Dave Day to move the *Solid Muldoon* from Ouray to Durango. Day, having stirred up a goodly amount of antipathy in Ouray through the years, agreed.

Mears had two preliminary surveys done to Phoenix through the Salt River Valley, and even though the country was in recession, he had no trouble raising enough capital to make a beginning. During 1892, while a third survey was being made of another route, Mears kept silent about his plans, and rumor in Colorado was rife. Mears was said to be building a Rio Grande Southern extension to Albuquerque, Phoenix, Flagstaff, Texas, Grand Junction, San Diego, or even Bluff, Utah, to take advantage of gold discoveries there. Finally, in early 1893, Mears announced his plans to take the extension to Phoenix and then on to San Diego. Had he been able to carry this out, the little Russian Jew who had arrived in this country without a penny might have become one of the richest railroad tycoons in our history. But this was not to be. The silver crash and national depression of 1893 devastated the Colorado economy. By September of 1893, half of the producing mines in Colorado had been forced to close, nearly 400 businesses had failed, and 45,000 persons were unemployed.

Mears' frantic efforts to stabilize his holdings made one thing clear — his Silverton Railroad was in no trouble. Most of the ore hauled by that line was copper ore or very high-grade silver, profitable at even half the former price. Though Mears might have to wait months for payment, the silver crash did not directly affect the Silverton line. Even though Red Mountain Town had burned in 1892 (a not-uncommon occurrence in those little wooden towns heated by wood stoves) and 500 people were made temporarily homeless, copper and high-grade silver ore production remained steady. The little town was rebuilt in just weeks.

The Rio Grande Southern, however, was hard hit. The lower-producing silver mines were closing, and Mears had to reduce staff, cut pay, and drop freight rates. Bank closures locked up or lost much of his funding. To raise money for expenses on the Southern, Mears had to sell much of the stock he held in other enterprises. Mears was finding himself unable to pay the interest on the investments that had built the Rio Grande Southern. To avert both bankruptcy and the possibility of eastern investors taking over the line, Mears petitioned the courts to put the Rio Grande Southern into receivership. The Denver and Rio Grande was appointed receiver because it held a large amount of the stock of the company. On August 3, 1893, the *Ridgway Herald* announced the dreadful news:

> *"The Southern in the Hands of a Receiver! Yesterday morning Superintendent Lee was informed that the Southern had gone into the hands of a receiver, the latter having been appointed to that position." Otto Mears was no longer in charge.*[16]

While unable to do much but wait on the economy to improve as far as the Southern was concerned, Mears occupied himself with the Silverton Railroad and the Standard Smelter in Durango, which was based on copper as well as high-grade silver ore.

Finally it became clear that silver mining in the San Juans was not going to be able to spring back soon enough or in enough volume to save the Rio Grande Southern. At one point, the company was a million dollars in debt. Mears and the other major stockholders agreed that the only answer was to sell it, and the Denver and Rio Grande wanted to buy it. This discouraging sale of the Rio Grande Southern in November 1895 was Mears' greatest financial setback.

The Rio Grande Southern struggled on, somehow being kept alive, for four more decades. David Lavender describes its condition twenty-five years after Mears sold it:

> *Railroading on the Southern requires patience and perseverance. In 1920, while escorting fifteen cars of cattle and six of apples over a rain-softened roadbed, head shack*

*J. H. Crum and his crew, using camel-back frogs and vit-
riolic language, overcame twenty-five separate derail-
ments during a single trip, twenty-two of them within one
six-mile stretch. On another occasion, when a cattle car
tipped over in a cut, the crew released the animals by chop-
ping a hole in the roof. Brand Inspector Seth Etheridge,
who happened to be along, walked to a nearby ranch, borrowed a horse, and drove the steers to Mancos, four miles
distant. Meanwhile the trainmen somehow hauled the
errant car back on the track, chugged into town, borrowed
a less damaged vehicle, reloaded the steers, and steamed
ahead, all within two hours.*[17]

By the early thirties, the Rio Grande Southern seemed on its death
bed, but it was rescued for a few more years by doubling its mail sub-
sidy, new labor contracts, heroic economies in operation and maintenance, and the institution of the nationally famous Galloping Goose, a
hybrid motor truck running on rails. With these efforts, the Rio Grande
Southern Railroad stayed operational until after World War II.

Meanwhile, Mears had further examined the surveys of 1889 and
1890 and decided to go ahead with the railway up the Animas River
from Silverton since the mines in that area produced large amounts of
gold. Late in the summer of 1895, he organized the Silverton Northern
Railroad Company. The Silverton Northern purchased Mears' Animas
Forks Toll Road bed, in return for giving Mears 1,494 of the 1,500 shares
of stock. Track was laid to Howardsville by late May 1896, and into
Eureka before the end of June. The final extension, to Animas Forks,
was not made until 1904. It has been said that the last part of the line
between Eureka and Animas Forks was so steep (perhaps as much as
a six percent grade) that a locomotive could haul only "two cars full,
three cars empty," and at that, the cars were *pushed* up the grade by the
engine for safety reasons.

In 1898 and 1899, Mears looked closely at developing a Silverton-
to-Gladstone line, but although it appeared to be a profitable proposi-
tion, Mears did not have the capital to do the construction, nor was he
able to raise it elsewhere. In 1899, others would develop that rail line.

Meanwhile, confident that financial conditions would improve in
the Red Mountain District, in the summer of 1899, Mears invested suf-
ficiently to upgrade his Silverton Railroad, replacing defective rails and

ties. Mears' information sources had failed him, however, because the Red Mountain mines that had been slated to reopen did not, and the few operating mines were closed by strikes of workers demanding shorter hours. The Silverton Railroad, after its great success, had been approaching dire financial straits. Now, unable to meet its expenses nor the interest due on its bonds, the Silverton went into receivership.

During and after his later development efforts with the Chesapeake Railway, Mears again sought to build an electric railway from Ouray to Ironton on his old toll road bed, and developed plans to extend the Silverton Northern to Lake City to meet the D&RG branch from Sapinero. Neither proposal proved viable.

In 1897, Mears accepted an offer from David Moffat, President of the Denver and Rio Grande Railroad and an investor in railroads in Colorado and elsewhere, to move back east to complete the Chesapeake Beach Railway between Washington, D.C. and Chesapeake Beach, Maryland. Mears did not abandon his San Juan railroads, leaving them in the good managerial hands of Alexander Anderson, and visiting them himself on a monthly basis. Faced not only with terrain and right-of-way difficulties in Maryland, Mears fought continual legal battles against others who wished to oust Mears and take over the East-Coast company. David Moffat himself eventually became one of Mears' strongest opponents, disagreeing with Mears' management decisions both financial and technical. Moffat bought up stock until in 1902, as majority stockholder, he could force Mears to resign, a severe blow to Mears' pride.

After closing out his Washington office, where, true to his nature, he had been involved in political life (including being on the committee to plan William McKinley's inaugural ball in 1901), Mears returned briefly to Colorado. In 1905, Moffat used legal means to make Mears sell his remaining stock in the Chesapeake, taking advantage of Mears' indebtedness to legally force Mears to liquidate. Mears lost not only his investment in the Chesapeake but his part of the profits which that railway would make over the next thirty years.

In 1903, finding that the Colorado economy had not really improved enough to justify more railroad investment, Mears became intrigued by a proposal to build a railway line between Monroe and New Iberia, Louisiana, a distance of 195 miles. Later it was decided to extend the road from New Iberia to New Orleans. The line would run through timbered country, and Mears also hoped to use the new line to ship timber from Louisiana to the mines above timberline in Colorado.

Concealing the fact that he remained a Republican Party boss in Colorado, Mears became what he called a "Louisiana Democrat" to support his business interests. The Louisiana state assembly granted him the charter for the Louisiana Central Railroad in early 1904. Mears oversaw construction, but the swampy terrain offered very different difficulties from the high mountain country in Colorado. The real blow came when a competitor beat out Mears in obtaining a right-of-way into New Orleans. The Louisiana Central became too costly for Mears and construction was stopped after only thirty-three miles of track had been laid. Nevertheless, the line began its shortened operation in 1907 and made a net profit over the next several years.

While living part-time in Louisiana, Mears became interested in the culture there, and was so taken with the Mardi Gras tradition that he volunteered to manage the celebration in 1905.

Through the early years of the twentieth century, Mears repeatedly tried to reorganize his railroads, particularly making the effort to use his profitable Silverton Northern to support the debt-ridden Silverton Railroad. By 1903 and 1904, the Silverton was running so rarely, and its debt was so heavy, that even with a successful reorganization to end the receivership of the Silverton, the line still had to be abandoned.

His worries about the Silverton at an end, and in a reasonable financial state, in 1905 Mears was able to extend a new branch of the Silverton Northern a mile and a half from Howardsville to the new Green Mountain Mill. In that same year, once again Mears' attentions turned to trying to run a line from Ouray to Ironton. The electric railway scheme had failed, but this time Mears turned to the idea of a cog railway. Again the expense of such a venture simply made it unfeasible, and the idea was dropped. Another failed plan was to use his "railway automobile" by laying track on his Ouray-to-Ironton Toll Road route.

Mears continued to investigate ideas that did not pan out — a Silverton Northern extension to Lake City, a scheme to build snow sheds strong enough to shield the Silverton Northern tracks to permit winter travel, and a branch from Animas Forks to Mineral Point.

Mears' activities again broadened when he became interested in the Mack Brothers Motor Car Company, which had been incorporated in 1905 in Allentown, Pennsylvania. Mears invested heavily and even became president of the Mack Company for nine months in 1905 and

1906. Mears ordered a "railroad automobile" to run on his narrow gauge lines in Colorado. He named the car the "Mary M." after his wife. The Mary M. was a true rail car and was equipped with a six-cylinder, ninety-horsepower gasoline engine. However, the Mary M. never made it to Silverton. After several months' display at Coney Island, it broke down on its maiden trip over Cumbres Pass on the D&RG line, and was sent to the shops at Alamosa for more work, but it never functioned well at Colorado altitudes. Two years later, continuing his desire to run a rail-road automobile on his narrow gauge lines, Mears built another model that would carry ten to twelve passengers. It had a four-cylinder, thirty-horsepower water-cooled engine. This car made it to Silverton in the summer of 1908 and Mears ran it around to the mountain villages every day for a week. It was never really more than a novelty, as it was unable to operate efficiently for long periods at those high altitudes.

After leaving his position at Mack and his Louisiana Central dreams had been blocked, Mears decided to "retire" to Colorado. He left subordinates in charge of the remaining work in Louisiana and returned to Colorado. Mears had lost a lot of money in the East, but he had not given up, and he immediately began to rebuild his fortune. Of course he had not neglected his railroad and mining interests in the San Juans even while he was busy in the East and South, and this provided his base on which to build.

In the summer of 1909, one of Mears' most important construction — or rather reconstruction — projects was just about to begin. Days of heavy rains that summer had caused rock- and mud-slides so great that all the railroads of the district suffered broken and washed out track and tons of debris on the remaining track. Supply lines to and from Silverton were cut off. Mears and his crews put his own lines in order, and then Mears offered their services to the Denver and Rio Grande. A contract was agreed to — a crew headed by Mears would work south out of Silverton towards Durango; the other crew, supervised by a D&RG manager, would work north.

The work proceeded well until about fifteen miles south of Silverton where the old track was covered by a gigantic rock fall. At Mears' suggestion, the crew left the fall. They simply built a new roadbed at a five percent grade on rock and earth piled ten feet deep over the old bed. Work continued south — clearing away numerous rockslides, rebuilding part of a bridge, grading miles of washed-out roadbed, and replacing track. On September 24, the two crews were able to cut through the largest rockslide of all and the following day, the forty-six-day blockade of Silverton was ended with a train steaming up from Durango with much needed supplies. Waiting at Silverton were eighty-three fully loaded cars of ore to be hauled back to the smelters at Durango. The people of Silverton gave Otto Mears a commemorative engraved silver punch bowl as well as celebrations and serenades from the townspeople and the Silverton Cornet Band.

This was not the end. Only weeks later, Telluride railroad traffic was shut off by a storm that washed away the Rio Grande Southern tracks. Food and fuel had to be freighted in at exorbitant rates, and winter was approaching. After some dithering and nothing being done, the Rio Grande Southern hired Mears and his crew to restore the roadbed. Two weeks of two ten-hour shifts each day restored the line, and Telluride honored Mears with a banquet and public reception where he was presented with an engraved decanter. Mears was nearly seventy years old at the time.

Not ready to retire and relax, in January 1910, Mears requested company stockholders' approval for a ten-year contract to lease the Silverton, Gladstone & Northerly Railroad. This was the line Mears had tried to build more than ten years before but had been unable to raise the funds. By 1910, the Gold King mine owners and the railroad owners believed that the mine was pretty well played out, and there would be little more ore to be mined and shipped. But Mears knew that in order to keep his earnings high on the Silverton Northern and other investments in the area, he had to keep the San Juan economy moving if he could.

In October of 1911 huge rains hit the region again, causing even greater destruction in some areas than had the rains of 1909. The Denver and Rio Grande, the Rio Grande Southern, and Mears' short lines were all hit with enormous destruction of track and equipment. Again Mears rallied his crew not only to repair his own lines but to contract with the D&RG to work on the line between Silverton and Durango. At seventy-one years of age, Mears' stamina and determination astonished others. He himself described his own workday during this effort:

> *I get up at 5:30 in the morning and at six I go to the depot, ready for starting work. The fresh air I get going to the depot, sometimes the temperature below zero and sometimes in a snowstorm, is very invigorating and tends*

to lengthen a man's life. This is especially true when I get down on the grade, where the men are often scattered over two or three miles and I take a walk over the line and then walk a couple of miles ahead with the Engineer, to lay the work for the next day and then return to the track-laying gang. By that time it is about lunch time and I take my dinner bucket and sit down on a rock or log and eat a hearty dinner, after which I rest until 12:45, which is our time for resuming work in the afternoon. To do this makes a man of my age feel good. Meantime my Asst. Supt. keeps walking up and down the line the whole day, telling the gang bosses that the salvation of Silverton lies in our getting through by Dec. 1st, and impressing it upon them that it will ruin the camp if we don't get through by that time.

Workers clear a snow slide from railroad track, by hand, with shovels.

The only trouble I have is getting a sufficient number of ties. When I get home between six or seven in the evening, I take a hot whisky toddy, eat my dinner, read the three day old papers and go to bed to dream about ties.[18]

David Lavender presents a colorful and descriptive report of this 1911 track repair:

Another flood ripped the Denver & Rio Grande's Animas Canyon tracks to shreds, and this time the disaster struck in October, just before the paralyzing fist of winter closed on the San Juans. Fear rippled through Silverton. Mines, merchants, and housewives had not yet laid in their winter supplies, and if blizzards struck before the rails were cleared, the town would be destitute.

By telegraph desperate Denver & Rio Grande officials in Denver beseeched Otto Mears to do what he could. By nightfall he had hired 250 men, and had brought down rolling stock and equipment from his own railroads. But there was one thing which neither his own depleted yards nor those of the Denver & Rio Grande could furnish. That was coal to keep the work trains running. Silverton's unreplenished coal bins were all but empty.

Mears toured the town, appealing to mills, to stores, to homeowners. "Give us your coal!" The people shivered. Emptying the bins at the mines meant stopping production; at home, the threat of freezing. And suppose the tracks weren't rebuilt in time? Suppose their last bits of fuel were burned to no avail? Suppose . . . .

But Silverton had faith in Otto Mears. The mines opened their doors; storekeepers sent hoarded coal in drayloads; children lugged it to the depot in sacks. White whiskers, frock coat and all, Otto climbed into the cab of the lead locomotive and roared down the canyon. For nine weeks his crew and another pushing up from Durango raced the weather. And they won. Supplies poured into Silverton in the nick of time, and winter became not a specter of terror but just one more season of deep snow and cold.[19]

Of course, Otto Mears' life was not all work and no play. He invented a "railroad bicycle" based on four rubber-tired wheels that would run on the tracks of the Silverton Northern narrow gauge railway. Placed on the wheels was a platform on which two stationary bicycles were affixed side by side. The cyclists would pedal the bicycles, and the bicycle chains would turn the two rear wheels. Several people found it quite entertaining to pedal themselves back and forth around Silverton.

Ruby Williamson, a biographer of Mears' who obtained a lot of stories from his family and friends, reports another happening with the Silverton Northern:

> *One summer a request came to Silverton for a great quantity of columbines for some national convention that was to be held in Denver. A "Columbine Special" train was run from Silverton to Animas Forks for the purpose of procuring them. Mears donated the use of the train, railroad men donated their services and townspeople donated their time. They gathered what they estimated to be 25,000. A hardware man supplied washtubs in which the flowers were packed and shipped. They went out of Silverton on flat cars but were transferred to box cars at Alamosa. The columbines reached Denver and were displayed in front of the* Denver Post *building.*[20]

Because of his age and the dwindling profits on his railroads, Mears was to spend his remaining nine summers in Colorado working to build investments for his retirement, much of that effort in mining.

Keep that Nugget and You'll Never be Poor

Roads, merchandising, freighting, railways, real estate, dealings with the Indians, and his ubiquitous presence on the political scene, occupied most of Otto Mears' time since arriving in Colorado. But the principal reason for the entry of the white man into Colorado, and more particularly the San Juans, was the mineral wealth to be found there. Mining became one of Mears' primary investments later in his life. Before that time, although he invested in a number of mining interests, his primary business efforts were in transportation. However, mining was the life and purpose of the San Juans, and Otto Mears was not one to stand aside where there was money to be made.

The exploration of the western United States, and in fact, most of the Americas was driven by the Europeans' quest for precious metals. From Columbus to Cortez and Coronado, and then to the rush to California in 1849, to Colorado in 1859, and to the San Juans a decade after that, the white man sought gold — and if he couldn't find gold he'd take silver and copper and other metals.

Gold and silver lodes are often associated with quartz and with other minerals such as pyrite — fool's gold — and a lead sulfide called galena or a zinc sulfide called sphalerite. Gold was most easily found after erosion had worn down lodes and the gold was removed by water and deposited in stream beds in its nugget form.

Placer mining for gold is relatively simple — the weight of the gold is used to settle it out in water from the surrounding material, whether in a pan or a sluice. Hard rock mining, however, was vastly more difficult, requiring intensive labor underground to drill, blast, tunnel, and haul out waste rock and valuable ore.

Mining conditions were dark, wet, and dangerous, and the work was physically exhausting. Before the invention of hydraulic drills in which the water would carry away the dust, miners continually breathed in the lung-destroying dust created by the drilling, dust made even worse when power drills were invented. Cave-ins were a constant threat. Many a man came to California, Nevada, and Colorado hoping to make his fortune with the discovery of a rich lode, only to spend his life, a life all too often cut short, laboring for others in the cramped, wet darkness of a hard rock mine.

Otto Mears was obviously a part of the world of mining from its beginnings in the San Juans, not only building roads to the mining districts, but supplying prospectors and miners with goods from his stores, much of them hauled by his transportation companies. His partner Enos Hotchkiss was responsible for some of the first Lake City mineral finds, discovered as Hotchkiss was improving Mears' Lake City road. In 1879, coal was found along his Marshall Pass Toll Road and Mears used it for a good profit, selling the seam with the right-of-way to the Denver and Rio Grande in 1881. But he didn't become very much involved in the silver and gold mines themselves until around 1886 when he used income from his transportation company and toll roads to lease the Buckeye Mine in Silver Lake Basin near Silverton for a small annual fee. The mine owners were badly in debt, and apparently not knowing whether there was still significant ore in the mine, saw this as a way to get out of their financial crisis. Mears' miners found extensive deposits and for a while his investment paid off handsomely, in spite of a large input of capital for wages, supplies, and equipment. There was, however, finally a decisive avalanche, and the mine was shut down as a complete loss in 1889.

In that same year, Mears and three Ouray mining men organized a mining firm with a million dollars in capital stock which would seek to extract silver ore from the Calliope Mine in the Paquin mining district of Ouray County. For more than a year, the Calliope was one of the largest ore producers in the region. A few months later, Mears leased the Comstock Mine on Brown Mountain. He made considerable profit, most of which he invested in building the Rio Grande Southern Railroad.[1]

In January 1892, Mears and O.P. Posey, a Ouray mining magnate and Silverton merchant, went together to purchase the C.H.C. and Black Hawk mines at Rico for $325,000. The Black Hawk was a spectacular producer for a few years, but within a decade the ore deposits had played out and it was no longer profitable. That same year, Mears bought stock in the San Juan Consolidated Gold Mining Company (which owned the Golconda Mine) and in the Last Chance Mine. By mid-1893 he owned a third share each of the Harvey, the Black Lemon, and the Little Maggie, all near Rico.

Mears began to look seriously into the idea of building another smelter in Durango, a plan he had examined with David Moffat in 1890, but which had not been financially feasible for him at that time. In 1892 he went east and talked eastern investors, many of whom had helped capitalize the Rio Grande Southern, into this new investment. Mears spent the spring of 1892 in Durango supervising construction of the Standard Smelter, which was primarily designed to handle copper ore.

Never staying still for long, Mears also invested in real estate in Rico, was part of a group that bought the First National Bank of Rico, and became a large stockholder in the Globe Express Company, a larger outgrowth of the Rio Grande Express Company.

Mears was less involved in mining investments for almost a decade, as he was occupied with his railroads and other business. However, if a profitable deal came along, Mears was sure to try to have a hand in it one way or another. But times were tough in the region the last decade of the nineteenth century. Mining in the San Juans had tottered along after the 1893 crash, and Mears did all that he could to keep his little railroads running and even profitable. The Silverton, in particular, was in a bad financial way. In 1900, Mears tried either to lease or to buy a silver mine in the Red Mountain district believing that if he could prove it profitable, the news would encourage other mining investors, and the consequent increase in ore production would make money for his struggling Silverton Railroad. However, he was unsuccessful in finding a mine at his price that he felt might provide sufficient yield. He also tried to get his friend and political protégé, Simon Guggenheim, to provide financial assistance to the Silverton line, but Guggenheim felt that he already had too much invested in the San Juans. When Otto Mears returned permanently from Maryland and Louisiana in 1906, he found that the obstacles to expansion of his transportation dreams were just too big to overcome. The economy and the geography simply prevented him from expanding his railroads.

In the summer of 1908 he leased the Iowa-Tiger Mine for three years. Many thought him crazy. The mine had recently been closed because it couldn't make money. It was heavily mortgaged, back interest on the loan was due, and its financial condition was so bad that its stock was essentially worthless. Mears understood that success in mining depended greatly on the work habits of the miners. He instituted an almost unheard-of scheme in the Iowa-Tiger — after selecting the best miners he could find, he offered them a share in the profits. The Iowa-Tiger began to show a profit again. By the summer of 1909, it was returning twenty percent a month on capital, producing mostly silver and lead. And on July 13, 1910, this profitable investment was turned into a bonanza by the foreman's discovery of a vein of gold. Twenty sacks of gold ore — worth $1,200 a ton — were extracted the first day. So much ore was eventually found that the Iowa-Tiger debts and mortgage were paid off and the formerly worthless stock began to pay a dividend. Although because of his lease, Mears had to pay large royalties to the owners, he was nevertheless able to repay the debts he had accumulated since 1893 and even to become a millionaire.

In August 1911, thirteen months after the Iowa-Tiger boom, Mears leased the Gold King Mine at Gladstone. He hoped this mine would provide enough ore to significantly increase business on the Silverton, Gladstone & Northerly Railroad, which he had leased early in 1910 but which had not made a profit since his lease began. The Gold King was in bad shape. Physically, the workings had been abandoned for so long a time that considerable repair had to be made even before mining proper could continue. The mine was unsafe and so was the associated mill. The miners' boardinghouses were unlivable. Mears had to pay $4,500 a month royalties whether the mine was making any money or not, so the required repairs were completed as quickly as he could push them through. Again, Mears instituted a profit-sharing plan with the miners, and again the best miners were included in the plan in exchange for their making the effort to encourage efficient work habits from their colleagues.

Early results from the mine were so discouraging that Mears' son-in-law, James Robertson Pitcher, Jr., convinced the owners to reduce the royalties. By the following summer, however, high-yield gold ore was found at all levels in the mine. After this discovery, six to eight carloads of ore were taken each day from the Gold King Mine — so much ore that the Silverton, Gladstone & Northerly, which Mears had leased in 1910, had to be reconditioned in order to carry it. In 1915, Mears convinced the stockholders of the Silverton Northern to purchase the Silverton, Gladstone & Northerly from its bankrupt owners, who were fighting other debts, at the foreclosure sale in Denver.

Ruby Williamson, in her biography of Mears, reports a story told to her by Mears' son-in-law, J. R. Pitcher, Jr., about Otto Mears and the Gold King:

In 1911 Mrs. Percy Airy's husband was working at the Gold King mill at Gladstone and they were living in a little cabin with almost no furniture and conveniences. One morning while she was washing, Percy came running in, saying he was bringing his Uncle Jack Slattery, Otto Mears, James Pitcher, and Louis Quarnstrom in for dinner. Flustered and dismayed were no words for it! At such a camp no fresh stuff was available, but she managed a dinner of ham, scalloped potatoes, and canned vegetables, biscuits with butter and jam, fresh canned mountain raspberries, cake and coffee. She had only two stool chairs and one of them was occupied by the wash-tub which Mears urged her not to move. She put one man on the other stool chair, two on the bed, and two in rockers. Being very young, only nineteen, she was so embarrassed she wouldn't sit down at the table. Everybody praised her dinner and she felt better. When Otto Mears left he presented her with a very rich piece of gold ore, about the size of a large orange, and told her if she'd always keep that she'd never be poor.[2]

In November 1911, Mears incorporated the Iowa-Tiger Mining Company to manage his mine leases and holdings, and in December of that year, he signed a lease to operate the Gold Prince Mine and Mill at Animas Forks. This investment did not turn out to be successful. The next year brought Mears a far more ambitious mining project.

Arthur R. Wilfley invented the Wilfley table in 1896. This invention, used in ore refining, was so successful that mines on several continents began to use it. The basic element of this device was a ridged flat surface, or "table," lying at a slight slant. By running water through crushed ore on the table, the heavier metals sank and were caught by the ridges, and the lighter material was washed away. By 1913, at the age of fifty-three, Wilfley had refined his invention to a level of efficiency that made him believe it would be profitable to use it to treat low-grade "tailings," that is, leftover material from old milling operations that had not been worth processing further with earlier technology. Wilfley found an innovative investor in Otto Mears, with the contacts to try out this process and the knowledge to supervise the attempt. Mears and Wilfley selected the old Silver Lake Mill as the most likely candidate in the area.

In the early 1890s, E. G. Stoiber had begun the Silver Lake operation. To refine ore from the mine, he built a stamp mill on the shore of Silver Lake, in a basin high above the Animas River northeast of

Silverton, at an altitude of 12,150 feet. Another mill was subsequently built almost 3,000 feet lower in altitude down in the valley and railway sidings from the Silverton Northern had been laid at this location. Stoiber made a fortune on his mine, but because of the limited technology of his time, tons of valuable tailings had been left in the lake. Guggenheim's American Smelting and Refining Company had bought the property, but by 1913 was eager to get rid of it. In October 1913, an agreement was reached and Mears contracted to lease the mine for six years.

Even before the lease was signed, Mears and Wilfley began building a sixty-by-forty-foot plant on the west bank of the Animas River next to the Silverton Northern tracks. The plant contained three of the largest Wilfley tables ever built by the inventor. The plant could process 500-600 tons of tailings in twenty-four hours. The tailings themselves were pumped out of the lake above using another new invention of Wilfley's still in development at that time, a sand pump. The pump was placed on a flatboat on Silver Lake. The sand and water mixture pumped out of the lake was sent down the natural formation of Arastra Gulch about two-thirds of a mile until it reached a cliff. From there, the sand and water plunged down a gorge 1,300 feet to the 10,700-foot level. Thence a flue carried the slurry to a dewatering plant, and then a series of flumes carried it to a pipe over the Animas River and finally to the mill.[3] By mid-August, 1914, the mill was working to capacity and profitably.

However in 1914, a new ore process called flotation was also introduced to the San Juans. Flotation used chemicals instead of the Wilfley table. Mears and John Slattery decided to remodel the old mill at the Gladstone Gold King Mine to experiment with flotation processing. This proved even more efficient and profitable than the Wilfley table, salvaging from sixty to ninety percent of the metal from the tailings. In 1915 Mears had Wilfley install the flotation equipment in the Silver Lake mill. Immediately, the mill began to show even higher profits, and by the end of 1918, the mill had shipped concentrates worth a total of $101,000.[4]

In mid-July of 1916, Mears, John Slattery, and J. R. Pitcher, Jr., leased the Mayflower Mine, located in Arastra Gulch below Silver Lake. This mine contained several valuable claims. Again, Otto Mears "struck it rich," according to Williamson:

> *When Mears and his associates assumed control of*
> *the mine, they hired a crew of miners to begin work at once*

in the upper tunnel. Within five months a body of ore worth $25,000 was found, a discovery so large that the Silverton Standard *predicted the mine would become one of the largest producers in the San Juans.*[5]

This was Mears' last new mining venture. In the four years until his retirement he continued to supervise his railroad and mining interests. A major source of his income was the new Silver Lake Mill. By 1917 some 80,000 tons of tailings had been processed in this mill, at a gross worth of approximately $250,000. Over a quarter of a million tons of tailings still remained to be processed, and to do this even more efficiently, the mill was again remodeled in 1917. By 1919, most of the recoverable tailings had been processed. Arthur Wilfley sold his share in the operation to Mears, Wilfley himself turning to the invention of the centrifugal pump that was to become the foundation of the Wilfley family fortune.

By this time, Mears, too, was ready to retire. His health was declining and the market value of metals fell precipitously after World War I. He was unable to sell his railroads for an acceptable amount, but he did sell his home of thirteen years in Silverton. In May 1920, he finally resigned from the Colorado Board of Capitol Managers, and that

A few buildings remain today outside the mines at Silver Lake, high above Silverton.

summer he returned to Silverton for a final time to terminate what mining leases he still held.

Only the Silverton Northern Railroad still made any kind of profit, but all Mears' short lines were in poor financial condition. In 1922, Mears applied to the Interstate Commerce Commission and the Colorado Public Utilities Commission to terminate service on the Silverton Railroad and tear up the track. Red Mountain mine owners strongly objected, but Mears received permission to abandon and dismantle the line. He continued to try to find a buyer, but in 1923 the order to dismantle was finally given, and Mears executed a quit claim deed to the San Juan County Commissioners to take over the roadbed and right of way. The tracks were not torn up until a couple of years later, and in 1926 the same contractor dismantled the track of the Silverton, Gladstone & Northerly. Mears' family, namely his daughter and son-in-law, Cora and James R. Pitcher, Jr., kept the Silverton Northern Railroad running, though not always profitably, into the 1940s.

The Ubiquitous Mr. Mears

Otto Mears was well known during his lifetime and for many years afterward because of his public life. But occasionally we get glimpses into his private life, into Mears the man instead of Mears the politician or Mears the road builder. A few tidbits gathered from here and there will help round out the picture of the man Otto Mears and his life in the San Juans.

Arthur Ridgway, the one-time superintendent of Mears' Rio Grande Southern Railroad and chief engineer of the Denver and Rio Grande Western Railroad, said of Mears:

> *Eccentric, visionary, impetuous, indefatigable, generous, human, sympathetic, charitable — all combined in one personality made it impossible to say that as a man he was this or that or the other . . . .Of his varied activities and accomplishments, Mr. Mears has little to say. I doubt if he knew himself all of the things in which he was interested and even had an active part. He, through his energy, made many fortunes and lost as many through his generosity and good will to others. It is difficult to say to just how many activities and projects he devoted his time and money. The number is legion.*[1]

Needless to say, this glowing opinion of Otto Mears is held by few historians today and was disputed by many people of his own time. Clearly Mears' motives, his actions, and the means by which he gained so many of his successes were not based just on selflessness and generosity. His accomplishments were many and varied, and they did contribute greatly to Colorado's early development. But Otto Mears was, as we have said before, out to make money and although he had limits below which he would not go, those limits may have been quite a bit lower than where many of us would draw them.

In a file of personal and business correspondence in the Colorado State Historical Society Library[2] is found a letter from Otto Mears to Thomas F. Walsh, the wealthy mine developer and politician who made a real fortune from the Camp Bird Mine and other mines in the Ouray Mining District. The letter is worth quoting in its entirety, as it provides an interesting view into the times, as well as into Otto Mears' way of dealing with people (especially important and wealthy people). It was written in December 1902 when Mears was still residing in Washington as well as Colorado.

Washington, D. C., Dec. 5th, 1902

Mr. Thos. F. Walsh,
  1416 N. Y. Ave., N. W.
  Washington, D. C.

My dear Mr. Walsh,
  Answering your letter of Dec. 4th, and referring to our conversation of yesterday relative to certain mean gossip which came to you about yourself, and of which I was given as author, I am very glad to note that you state you did not believe it, for the reason that I have tried my best to recall any word or action of mine which could have possibly given rise to the talk of which you complain, and I can not think of anything I have said that could by any means have been construed into mean gossip about you or that could have hurt your feelings. On the contrary I have always spoken in the highest terms of you as a man. The only time I can remember having heard your name brought up in anything like a gossipy manner was once among a party of men some allusion was made to you in connection with a certain New York newspaper item, and immediately after my conversation with you yesterday I went to see one of the gentlemen who was present at that time and asked him if he recalled the conversation. He said he distinctly remembered it, and that when this newspaper item was referred to by some gentlemen present, I said, "all bosh; there is nothing in it."

If a so-called friend of yours informed you of the things which were alleged to have been said, I have to say in this connection that I consider him a very poor friend who would be willing to wound your feelings by telling you of disagreeable things, even if they were true. This friend must have had some "ax to grind" and was probably trying to court your favor or else he was trying to get money out of you.

You must know that a man of your position is always more or less subject to gossip and the only way to treat such reports is to pass them by unnoticed. Sometime ago a so-called friend of mine came to me and began to tell me some story he had heard about me and I told him to go to the devil, that I took no stock in any such stuff and did not want to hear it. I found out at the same time that this "friend" had some favors to ask and sought to enlist my aid by manufacturing gossip.

I do not think I ever had the reputation of talking about a man behind his back. On the contrary I think it has always been said of me that when I had anything against a man I would go straight to him with it, and he would always be the first man to hear it regardless of what it might be.

I desire to state further that my object in writing this letter is not to court any favors from you as I have no favors to ask and do not expect to have any. I do not, however, wish to be placed in a false light before any man. Inasmuch as you did not give me any definite information as to what the gossip was, nor when, where or to whom it was alleged to have been said, I can only deny it in this general way. I expect to leave tomorrow for Colorado, and should this letter not be sufficient, I will be glad upon my return to write you further on the subject, should you care to specify names and date.

With kind regards to yourself and family, I remain,
Yours very truly,
(s) Otto Mears

Today we show considerably more skepticism and, we hope, more attention to fact, than in some early reports. We know that Mears was both visionary and scoundrel, by our standards at least, and often by the standards of his day. Nevertheless, it is intriguing to read some of the gushing compliments given Mears in earlier times. For example, in the *History of Colorado*[3] from 1919:

> *While the state of Colorado has existence the name of Otto Mears will be an honored one within its borders because of the important part which he has played in its development. He has penetrated into its mountain fastnesses and broken paths across its plains. As a builder of toll roads and railroads he has contributed in marked measure to the task of opening up the state for settlement and he is most appropriately called the pathfinder of the San Juan . . . .*
>
> *It seems that no phase of Mr. Mears' intensely active business life was without its attendant public benefit . . . .The chance for development touched a responsive chord in him, as progress has ever been his watchword.*

And perhaps most egregiously, from the same source:

> *He has never sought to fill political positions, content to do his public service as a private citizen.*

Mears was known in his own time as the "ubiquitous Mr. Mears." A curious little item from the *Denver Times* in October 1899 reports:

> *Like a shadow, the Ubiquitous Otto Mears has come and returned to Washington from his monthly visit to Denver. Mr. Mears left last night, but before going he showed, on the quiet to his friends, his commission appointing him a member of the metropolitan police force in the capitol city of the United States.*

He had been appointed, with others, as part of a special guard for the parade in Washington honoring Admiral George Dewey, who had defeated the Spanish fleet in Manila Bay during the Spanish-American

War. It was an honorary position, but a regular signed commission. Mears enjoyed the recognition.

It may seem startling that in spite of all Otto Mears did for the state of Colorado, and the fame that he had during his lifetime, so little remains to remind present-day residents and visitors of the role he played. During his lifetime, Mears seemed content to stay more or less in the background. He certainly played power politics, and apparently very well, but he didn't seem to seek high office or fame for himself. Otto Mears was a businessman first, and although he did many creative things, business was always his primary motivation. Perhaps he would not be too upset now that he is not very well remembered, as that was not what he primarily sought.

The library of the Colorado Historical Society in Denver has a copy of Mears' application for an "invalid pension" as a "Discharged Soldier," what we would call a veteran. The application is dated December 25, 1906, and requests the pension on the basis of "old age." On the form is written, "He waives medical examination and respect-fully requests that his claim for pension be adjudicated on his age alone." One can see why he asked to have no medical examination on his application for a pension as an "invalid" — this is a man who five years later, in 1911, at the age of seventy-one, was spending long days on site helping with the enormous task of freeing the Denver and Rio

Otto Mears' last home in Silverton as it appears today.

Grande Railroad tracks from the devastation of mud and rock slides. One suspects that a medical examination would have spoiled his case. At any rate, based solely on his age and service with the Union Army at the end of the Civil War, Mears got his pension.

Much later, in July 1930, when Mears was in a nursing home in California and his daughter Cora filed for guardianship for her father as "an incompetent person," she lists his Army pension as $65.00 per month. Incidentally, she also states that "The pension referred to, constitutes practically all of his income." This seems unlikely, especially since Cora and her husband, J.R. Pitcher, Jr., were still involved in running Mears' businesses in Colorado.

Otto Mears' mining and milling operations in the San Juans were interrupted in 1913 when Mary's declining health forced him to take her to California where she was established in the Hotel Maryland in Pasadena. Otto and Mary had been spending winters there for some time; now Mary needed to be there year-round.

In a letter to Ruby Williamson, Otto Mears Pitcher, Mears' grandson, wrote about Otto and Mary Mears at this time:

> *My grandmother was a very gentle person, but nevertheless, her word was law. Early on, she became what might be called a health food "nut." Although the dining room of the Maryland Hotel in Pasadena where they were living served the rich and varied food of the period, her idea of a proper dinner consisted of a green salad, some fresh fruit and a few nuts. Grandfather went along with this regimen meekly enough, but after dinner, while my grandmother was visiting with friends in the hotel lobby, he would go for a walk — which led him across the street to a restaurant where he would enjoy a lobster or a steak followed by his favorite dessert: a double helping of vanilla ice-cream with roquefort cheese crumbled over it. And grandmother never the wiser.[5]*

In the warmer climate and lower altitude, Mary improved and Mears was able to return to Silverton in the summer of 1914.

On June 22, 1914, a blow hit Otto Mears — his long-time friend, newspaper editor David Frakes Day, died in Durango. The funeral was conducted in Denver, and Mears came from California to give a graveside tribute to his friend.

Another tragedy interrupted Mears' life soon thereafter. He missed the opening of the Silver Lake flotation plant because his oldest daughter, Laura, died of a brain tumor in June 1915 in Seattle. Although she had been in ill health, no one expected her death. Mears was devastated. At her prior request, Laura was cremated, and Mears brought her ashes to scatter them in the San Juan Mountains.

Otto and Mary Mears, late in their lives. They were married fifty-four years, until Mary's death in 1924.

Mary's health continued to suffer, and after a long decline, she died August 6, 1924. Otto and Mary had been married fifty-four years, and though he sometimes had a reputation as a ladies' man, he remained her companion and supporter through all those years. He spent the next two years grieving deeply.

In 1926, Mears decided to visit Colorado once again, in spite of his health problems and the high altitude. He remained in Silverton only a couple of weeks, having developed pneumonia from a cold he'd caught on the way out from California, and he was driven back home by his third grandson, Otto Mears Pitcher.

David Frakes Day had proposed as early as 1909 that a monument to Mears be placed at Sheridan Junction, near Red Mountain Town, to honor the old road builder. For almost a decade after Day's death, the monument idea lay dormant, until it was re-ignited by Day's son, Rod S. Day, who had taken over the *Durango Democrat*. Rod Day suggested that the monument be placed over Bear Creek Falls, perhaps the most spectacular point on Mears' toll road that later became U.S. Highway 550. Nothing much happened until 1924, when the *Silverton Standard* took up the call for some kind of memorial and began a subscription drive.

By 1926 sufficient funds had been collected and the monument was constructed in the form of a Salida granite tablet four feet high, three feet wide, and eight inches thick. The tablet was engraved with the words:

In honor of
OTTO MEARS
Pathfinder of the San Juan
Pioneer Road Builder
Built this Road in 1881

Erected by a Grateful People
1926

The monument was erected with great ceremony, although Mears himself was not able to be present. He visited the site in 1929 at the age of eighty-nine. Unfortunately, the monument was removed a few years later when it was damaged by a highway construction crew, and was not replaced in its former spot on U.S. Highway 550 until September 26, 1970.

Mears' 1929 trip was his last to Colorado. In the spring of 1930 his health, both mental and physical, began to fail rapidly. By May 1930 his daughter Cora Mears Pitcher had Mears placed in the Kimball Sanitarium in La Crescenta, California, and in June she applied for guardianship and custody of his affairs. According to Michael Kaplan, by this time Mears had distributed most of his assets to his heirs. He kept a real estate lot in Durango and continued to receive his Civil War pension. Mears was not yet ready, however, to give up management control over the family busi-

IN HONOR OF
OTTO MEARS
PATHFINDER OF THE SAN JUAN
PIONEER ROAD BUILDER
BUILT THIS ROAD IN 1881

ERECTED BY A GRATEFUL PEOPLE
1926

LOIS MONARREZ

In 1929, Otto Mears visited the memorial tablet erected in his honor at Bear Creek Falls.

ness interests. His distribution of assets was designed to avoid the necessity for a will. "The old timer was profoundly distrustful of lawyers and would do anything to avoid hiring one."[6]

In spite of his failing condition, Otto Mears' strong constitution kept him going until June 24, 1931. His remains were cremated two days later.

In accordance with his wishes, Cora took both Otto Mears' and his wife Mary's ashes to Silverton in August. An official day of mourning in Silverton was declared and memorial services were conducted at St. John's Episcopal Church on Snowden Street in Silverton, led by Episcopal Bishop Fred Ingley.

Perhaps the old pioneer had a last laugh, for controversy followed him even after death. Mears' ashes were variously said to have been taken to Eureka and scattered near the old Silverton Northern Railroad line, scattered at Bear Creek, scattered somewhere near Ouray, or scattered over Engineer Mountain.

In 1943 a Liberty ship built at the Naval yard in Richmond, California, was named after Mears, and there is 13,496-foot peak on the Ouray-San Miguel County line that bears his name. Other than that, Otto Mears has almost faded into obscurity.

Otto Mears was a visionary, but also a man of his times. He was forward thinking in employment and treatment of his workers, but he fought with every crooked political means at hand to defeat unionization of Colorado mines and railroads. Mears was one of the very few white men fluent in the Ute language, a good friend of Chief Ouray, and apparently well liked by the Utes, yet he was instrumental in their removal from Colorado. He was a road builder and railroad builder, yet was defeated in his long dream to put rails in from Ouray to Ironton, and he lost the Rio Grande Southern Railroad and the Silverton Railroad to receivership. He made and lost several fortunes. In his day he was called a governor-maker, but he died in relative obscurity in a nursing home in California.

It is well, perhaps, to remember Otto Mears, the builder of so much of the Colorado transportation system, simply as who he was, neither saint nor sinner, but just an adventurous, energetic man who dreamed dreams and made many of them come true.

NOTES

Introduction
[1] Quoted in Williamson, *Otto Mears*, p. 3.
[2] Uchill, *Pioneers, Peddlers, and Tsadikim*, p. 67.
[3] *Pioneers of the San Juan Country*, Vol. 1, pp. 15-17.

Chapter 1 — Work or Get Out
[1] *Pioneers of the San Juan Country*, Vol. 1, p. 15.
[2] Kaplan, *Otto Mears: Paradoxical Pathfinder*, p. 3.
[3] Ibid., p. 4.
[4] *Pioneers of the San Juan Country*, Vol. 1, p. 17.
[5] Quoted in Kushner, *Otto Mears: His Life and Times*, p. 8.
[6] Lavender, *The Big Divide*, p. 93.

Chapter 2 — That Pyramid of Enterprise
[1] *Pioneers of the San Juan Country*, Vol. 1, p. 18.
[2] Horgan, Paul, *Lamy of Santa Fe*, p. 335.
[3] *Pioneers of the San Juan Country*, Vol. 1, p. 18.
[4] Kaplan, *Otto Mears: Paradoxical Pathfinder*, p. 6.
[5] Quoted in Kaplan, *Otto Mears: Paradoxical Pathfinder*, p. 6.
[6] Kaplan, *Otto Mears: Paradoxical Pathfinder*, p. 21.
[7] Martin, *Frontier Eyewitness*, p. 83.
[8] Feitz, *Creede*, p. 26.
[9] Ellis, *The Life of an Ordinary Woman*, p. 25.
[10] Ibid., p. 37.
[11] James Robertson Pitcher, Jr., Mears' son-in-law, quoted in Black, *Otto Mears*, p. 9.
[12] Ellis, *The Life of an Ordinary Woman*, p. 37.
[13] Tarbell, Charles, quoted in Black, *Otto Mears*, p. 17.
[14] Kaplan, *Otto Mears: Paradoxical Pathfinder*, p. 19.
[15] Uchill, *Pioneers, Peddlers, and Tsadikim*, p. 53.

[16] Ibid.
[17] Ellis, *The Life of an Ordinary Woman*, p. 8.
[18] Martin, *Frontier Eyewitness*.
[19] Ibid., p. 35.
[20] Ibid., p. 73.
[21] Simmons, *The San Luis Valley*, p. 216.
[22] Ibid.
[23] Martin, *Frontier Eyewitness*, p. 85.
[24] Ibid.
[25] Dyer, *Snow-Shoe Itinerant*, pp. 205-206.
[26] Martin, *Frontier Eyewitness*, p. 25.
[27] Smith, P.D., *Ouray Chief of the Utes*, p. 118.
[28] Martin, *Frontier Eyewitness*, p. 85.
[29] Kushner, *Alferd G. Packer*, p. 133.
[30] Kushner, *Otto Mears: His Life and Times*, p. 65.
[31] The *Denver Post*, date unknown, quoted in Kushner, *Alferd G. Packer*, p. 268.

Chapter 3 — The Toll Road King
[1] Quoted from Mears' memoirs in Black, *Otto Mears*, p. 7.
[2] Kaplan, *Otto Mears: Paradoxical Pathfinder*, p. 10.
[3] Williamson, *Otto Mears*, p. 66.
[4] Quoted in Sprague, *The Great Gates*, pp. 256-257.
[5] Brown, Robert L., *An Empire of Silver*, pp. 151-152.
[6] Quoted from Mears' memoirs in Williamson, *Otto Mears*, p. 74.
[7] Williamson, *Otto Mears*, p. 58.
[8] Smith, P. D., *Mountains of Silver*, p. 100.
[9] Quoted in Brown, Robert L., *An Empire of Silver*, p. 162.
[10] Martin, *Frontier Eyewitness*, p. 92.
[11] Brown, Robert L., *An Empire of Silver*, pp. 161-162.
[12] Reyher, *Silver & Sawdust*, p. 37.
[13] Kaplan, *Otto Mears: Paradoxical Pathfinder*, p. 16.
[14] Quoted in Kaplan, *Otto Mears: Paradoxical Pathfinder*, p. 18.
[15] Martin, *Frontier Eyewitness*, p. 99.

[16] Quoted in Kaplan, *Otto Mears: Paradoxical Pathfinder*, p. 33.
[17] Sprague, *The Great Gates*, p. 252.
[18] Quoted in Williamson, *Otto Mears*, pp. 70-71.
[19] Ibid., p. 71.
[20] Quoted from Mears' memoirs in Williamson, *Otto Mears*, p. 67.
[21] Quoted in Kaplan, Michael D., "The Toll Road Building Career of Otto Mears."
[22] Sloan and Skowronski, *The Rainbow Route*, p. 20.
[23] Massard, Frank, "Memoirs," *Ouray County Plaindealer*, Oct. 16, 1980.
[24] Kaplan, *Otto Mears: Paradoxical Pathfinder*, p. 64.
[25] Kaplan, "The Toll Road Building Career of Otto Mears."
[26] Smith, P.D., *Mountains of Silver*, p. 93.
[27] Martin, *Frontier Eyewitness*, p. 31.

Chapter 4 — Speaking Ute with a Heavy Russian Accent
[1] Kaplan, *Otto Mears: Paradoxical Pathfinder*, p. 32.
[2] Smith, P. D., *Ouray, Chief of the Utes*, p. 84.
[3] Martin, *Frontier Eyewitness*, p. 38.
[4] Marsh, *People of the Shining Mountains*, p. 69.
[5] Quoted in Smith, P.D., *Ouray, Chief of the Utes*, p. 91; no date given.
[6] Smith, P. D., *Ouray, Chief of the Utes*, p. 103.
[7] Quoted in Brown, Dee, *Bury My Heart at Wounded Knee*, p. 387.
[8] Kaplan, *Paradoxical Pathfinder*, pp. 33-35.
[9] Martin, *Frontier Eyewitness*, p. 72.
[10] Marsh, *People of the Shining Mountains*, p. 75.
[11] Brown, *Bury My Heart at Wounded Knee*, p. 370.
[12] Quoted in Black, *Otto Mears*, p. 47.
[13] Williamson, *Otto Mears*, p. 49.
[14] Quoted from Mears' memoirs in Black, *Otto Mears*, p. 48.
[15] Ubbelohde, *A Colorado History*, p. 188.
[16] The *Pueblo Tribune*, quoted in Williamson, *Otto Mears*, p. 49.
[17] Ibid., p. 50.

[18] Smith, P. D., *Ouray, Chief of the Utes*, p. 186.
[19] Quoted in Smith, P. D., *Ouray, Chief of the Utes*, pp. 187-189.
[20] Ibid., p. 189.
[21] Jocknick, *Early Days on the Western Slope*, p. 225.
[22] Schneider, "Otto Mears — Pathfinder of the San Juans."
[23] Jocknick, *Early Days on the Western Slope*, p. 192.
[24] *Pueblo Chieftain*, January 11, 1959, "Otto Mears Built Toll Roads into San Juans."
[25] Kaplan, *Otto Mears: Paradoxical Pathfinder*, p. 51.
[26] Ewegen, Bob, "Two Bucks for a Birthright," *Denver Post*, July 14, 1997, p. unk.
[27] Ibid.
[28] Dawson Scrap Books, July 5, 1993, Vol. 62, p. 357.
[29] Unidentified newspaper account in the Archives of the Silverton History Museum, Silverton, Colorado.

Chapter 5 — Joker in the Republican Deck
[1] Martin, *Frontier Eyewitness*, p. 52.
[2] Ibid., p. 52.
[3] Ubbelohde, *A Colorado History*, p. 218.
[4] Kaplan, *Otto Mears: Paradoxical Pathfinder*, p. 24.
[5] Ibid., pp. 50-51.
[6] Ibid., pp. 89-90.
[7] Hunt and Draper, *To Colorado's Restless Ghosts*, pp. 292.
[8] Quoted in Kaplan, *Otto Mears: Paradoxical Pathfinder*, p. 91.
[9] Kaplan, *Otto Mears: Paradoxical Pathfinder*, p. 93.
[10] Ibid., p. 95.
[11] Quoted in the *Denver Times*, "Was it Bribery?" April 14, 1891.
[12] Ibid.
[13] Kaplan, *Otto Mears: Paradoxical Pathfinder*, p. 140.
[14] Quoted in Williamson, *Otto Mears*, pp. 95-96.
[15] Quoted in Kaplan, *Otto Mears: Paradoxical Pathfinder*, p. 159.
[16] Kaplan, *Otto Mears: Paradoxical Pathfinder*, p. 172.

NOTES

[17] Quoted in Williamson, *Otto Mears*, p. 102.

[18] Quoted in Kaplan, *Otto Mears: Paradoxical Pathfinder*, p. 185.

[19] Kaplan, *Otto Mears: Paradoxical Pathfinder*, p. 186.

[20] Quoted in Kaplan, *Otto Mears: Paradoxical Pathfinder*, p. 188.

Chapter 6 — Audacious Little Narrow-Gauge Lines

[1] Sloan and Skowronski, *The Rainbow Route*, p. 6.

[2] Smith, Duane, *Song of the Hammer and Drill*, p. 71.

[3] Kaplan, *Otto Mears: Paradoxical Pathfinder*, pp. 69-70.

[4] Reyher, *Silver & Sawdust*, p. 27.

[5] Ibid., p. 47.

[6] Sprague, *The Great Gates*, p. 280.

[7] Quoted in Kaplan, *Otto Mears: Paradoxical Pathfinder*, p. 73.

[8] Black, "Corkscrew Gulch Turntable" (see Bibliography).

[9] Ibid.

[10] Quoted in Crum, *Three Little Lines*, p. 6.

[11] Quoted in Kaplan, *Otto Mears: Paradoxical Pathfinder*, p. 78.

[12] Sloan and Skowronski, *The Rainbow Route*, p. 36.

[13] Collman, *The RGS Story*, Vol. 1, pp. 20-21.

[14] Ibid., Vol. I, p. 7.

[15] Quoted in Kaplan, *Otto Mears: Paradoxical Pathfinder*, p. 106.

[16] Gregory, *History of Ouray*, p. 88.

[17] Lavender, *The Big Divide*, pp. 178-179.

[18] Personal letter of Otto Mears to J. B. Andrews, quoted in Kaplan, *Otto Mears: Paradoxical Pathfinder*, pp. 233-234.

[19] Lavender, David, "Skyline Engineer," *Rocky Mountain Empire Magazine*, December 5, 1948, p. 2.

[20] Williamson, *Otto Mears*, pp. 86-87.

Chapter 7 — Keep that Nugget and You'll Never be Poor

[1] Kaplan, *Otto Mears: Paradoxical Pathfinder*, pp. 99-100.

[2] Williamson, *Otto Mears*, p. 86.

[3] Niebur, *Arthur Redman Wilfley*, p. 158.

[4] Ibid., p. 166.

[5] Williamson, *Otto Mears*, p. 245.

Chapter 8 — The Ubiquitous Mr. Mears

[1] Sloan and Skowronski, *The Rainbow Route*, p. 35.

[2] Colorado Historical Society, Stephen H. Hart Library.

[3] *History of Colorado*, pp. 640-641.

[4] Colorado Historical Society, Stephen H. Hart Library.

[5] Quoted in Williamson, *Otto Mears*, p. 116.

[6] Ibid., p. 264.

BIBLIOGRAPHY

ALDRICH, John K., *Ghosts of the Western San Juans*, Vol. 1. Centennial Graphics, Lakewood, Colorado, 1998.

BECK, Warren A., and HAASE, Ynez D., *Historical Atlas of New Mexico.* University of Oklahoma Press, Norman, Oklahoma, 1969.

BENHAM, Jack L., *Camp Bird and the Revenue.* Bear Creek Publishing Company, Ouray, Colorado, 1980.

BLACK, Carla F., "Corkscrew Gulch Turntable," *Railroad Model Craftsman*, March 1989, pp.61-68.

BRIGGS, Asa, ed., *The Nineteenth Century.* McGraw-Hill Book Company, London, 1970.

BROWN, Dee, *Bury My Heart at Wounded Knee: An Indian History of the American West.* Holt, Rinehart & Winston, New York, 1970.

BROWN, Robert L., *An Empire of Silver: A History of the San Juan Silver Rush.* The Caxton Printers., Ltd., Caldwell, Idaho, 1965.

COLLMAN, Russ, and MCCOY, Dell A., *The R.G.S. Story: Rio Grande Southern*, Vol. I, *Over the Bridges . . . Ridgway to Telluride;* Vol. II, *Telluride, Pandora and the Mines Above;* and Vol. III (with William A. Graves), *Over the Bridges . . . Vance Junction to Ophir.* Sundance Publications, Ltd., Denver, 1990.

CRUM, Josie Moore, *The Rio Grande Southern Railroad.* San Juan History, Durango, Colorado, 1961.

CRUM, Josie Moore, *Three Little Lines. Durango Herald-News,* Durango, Colorado, 1960.

The DAWSON Scrapbooks, an extensive collection of clippings and articles, held by the Stephen H. Hart Library of the Colorado Historical Society, 1300 Broadway, Denver, Colorado.

DUNN, J. P., Jr., *Massacres of the Mountains: A History of the Indian Wars of the Far West — 1815-1875.* Archer House, Inc., New York, reprint of the 1886 edition.

DYER, John L., *Snow-Shoe Itinerant.* Father Dyer United Methodist Church reprint of the 1889 edition, Breckenridge, Colorado, 1975.

ELLIS, Anne, *The Life of an Ordinary Woman.* University of Nebraska Press, reprint of the Houghton Mifflin Co. 1929 edition, Lincoln, Nebraska, 1987.

FEITZ, Leland, *Creede, Colorado Boom Town.* Little London Press, Colorado Springs, Colorado, 1969.

GREGORY, Doris H., *History of Ouray: A Heritage of Mining and Everlasting Beauty,* Vol. 1. Cascade Publications, Ouray, Colorado, 1995.

GREGORY, Marvin, and SMITH, P. David, *The Million Dollar Highway.* Wayfinder Press, Ouray, Colorado, 1986.

History of Colorado (no author), Vol. IV. S. J. Clarke Publishing Company, Chicago, 1919.

HORGAN, Paul, *Lamy of Santa Fe: His Life and Times.* Farrar, Straus and Giroux, New York, 1975.

HUNT, Inez, and DRAPER, Wanetta, *To Colorado's Restless Ghosts.* Sage Books, Alan Swallow, Denver, 1960.

JOCKNICK, Sidney, *Early Days on the Western Slope of Colorado and Campfire Chats with Otto Mears, the Pathfinder, from 1870 to 1883 Inclusive.* Western Reflections, Inc., reprint of the 1913 edition, Ouray, Colorado, 1998.

KAPLAN, Michael, *Otto Mears: Paradoxical Pathfinder.* San Juan Book Company, Silverton, Colorado, 1982.

KAPLAN, Michael D., "The Toll Road Building Career of Otto Mears, 1881-1887, *Colorado Magazine*, State Historical Society of Colorado Quarterly, Vol. 52, No. 2, Spring 1975, pp. 153-170.

KUSHNER, Ervan, *Otto Mears, His Life and Times, with Notes on the Alferd Packer Case.* Jende-Hagen Book Corporation, The Platte N Press, Frederick, Colorado, 1979.

KUSHNER, Ervan F., *Alferd G. Packer, Cannibal! Victim?* Platte N Press, Frederick, Colorado, 1980.

LAVENDER, David, *The Big Divide.* Doubleday & Company, Inc., Garden City, New York, 1948.

LAWRENCE, John, *A History of Russia.* Mentor Books, New American Library, New York, 1962.

MARSH, Charles S., *People of the Shining Mountains: The Utes of Colorado.* Pruett Publishing Company, Boulder, Colorado, 1982.

MARSHALL, John, with ZANONI, Zeke, *Mining in the Hard Rock.* Simpler Way Book Company, Silverton, Colorado, 1996.

MARTIN, Bernice, ed., *Frontier Eyewitness: Diary of John Lawrence, 1867-1908.* The Saguache County Museum, Saguache, Colorado, no date.

NIEBUR, Jay E., *Arthur Redman Wilfley: Miner, Inventor, Entrepreneur.* Western Business History Research Center, Colorado Historical Society, Denver, no date given.

NOLAND, James M., *The First 50 Years of Electra Sporting Club, 1910-1960.* Pamphlet held in the Stephen H. Hart Library of the Colorado Historical Society, 1300 Broadway, Denver, Colorado.

NOSSAMAN, Allen, *Many More Mountains,* Volume 1: *Silverton's Roots;* Volume 2: *Ruts into Silverton;* Volume 3: *Rails into Silverton.* Sundance Publications, Ltd., Denver, 1998.

PARKER, E. S., Commissioner, *Annual Report of the Commissioner of Indian Affairs to the Secretary of the Interior for the Year 1870,* to the Hon. J. D. Cox, Secretary of the Interior, U. S. Government Printing Office, Washington, D.C.

Pioneers of the San Juan Country. Sara Platt Decker Chapter, D.A.R., Durango Colorado, Vol. I, 1942; Vol. II, 1946; Vol. III, 1952; Vol. IV, 1962.

REED, Verner Z., T*he Southern Ute Indians of Early Colorado.* Originally published in *The California Illustrated Magazine* for 1893, Reprint by Outbooks, Golden, Colorado, 1980.

REYHER, Ken, *Silver & Sawdust: Life in the San Juans.* Western Reflections Publishing Company, Ouray, Colorado, 2000.

ROCKWELL, Wilson, *The Utes, A Forgotten People.* Sage Books, Denver, 1956.

ROCKWELL, Wilson, *Uncompahgre Country.* Sage Books, Denver, 1965.

ROTH, David E., *The Civil War 1861-1865.* Smithmark Publishers, Inc., New York, 1992.

SCHNEIDER, James G., "Otto Mears — Pathfinder of the San Juans," in *The Westerners Brand Book,* Vol. XXXI, Number 11-12, January-February, 1975.

SELIGSON, Harry, and BARDWELL, George E., *Labor-Management Relations in Colorado.* Sage Books, Denver, 1961.

SIMMONS, Virginia McConnell, *The San Luis Valley: Land of the Six-Armed Cross,* 2nd edition. University Press of Colorado, Niwot, Colorado, 1999.

SLOANE, Robert E., and SKOWRONSKI, Carl A., *The Rainbow Route: An Illustrated History.* Sundance Publications Limited, Denver, 1975.

SMITH, Duane, in the Foreword to Jocknick, Sidney, *Early Days on the Western Slope* (see above).

SMITH, Duane, *Song of the Hammer and Drill, the Colorado San Juans, 1860-1914.* University Press of Colorado, Boulder, Colorado, 2000.

SMITH, P. David, *Images of the San Juans — Historical Selections from the Ruth and Marvin Gregory Photograph Collection.* Western Reflections, Inc., Ouray, Colorado, 1977.

SMITH, P. David, *Mountains of Silver: The Story of Colorado's Red Mountain Mining District.* Pruett Publishing Company, Boulder, Colorado, 1994.

SMITH, P. David, *Ouray, Chief of the Utes.* Wayfinder Press, Ridgway, Colorado, 1990.

SPRAGUE, Marshall, *The Great Gates: The Story of the Rocky Mountain Passes.* Little, Brown and Company, Boston, 1964.

STRONG, William K., *The Remarkable Railroad Passes of Otto Mears.* San Juan County Book Company, Silverton, Colorado, 1988.

TWAIN, Mark, *Roughing It.* New American Library, Penguin, Inc., New York, 1980.

UBBELOHDE, Carl, BENSON, Maxine, and SMITH, Duane A., eds., *A Colorado History.* Pruett Publishing Company, Boulder, Colorado, 1982.

UCHILL, Ida Libert, *Pioneers, Peddlers, and* Tsadikim*: The Story of the Jews in Colorado.* Quality Line Printing Co., Boulder, Colorado, 1957.

WILLIAMSON, Ruby G., *Otto Mears, "Pathfinder of the San Juan": His Family and Friends.* B&B Printers, Gunnison, Inc., Gunnison, Colorado, 1981.

INDEX

CPSIA information can be obtained
at www.ICGtesting.com
Printed in the USA
LVHW051300020721
691628LV00008B/132

9 781890 437855